NAPKIN FOLDING

NAPKIN FOLDING

Gay Merrill Gross ♦ Photography by Michael Grand

Friedman Group

To the best of the publisher's knowledge, all the napkin folds in this book, unless otherwise credited, are traditional designs.

The publisher would like to thank the following people for supplying the items seen in the photographs: most napkins were supplied by "Now Designs," which can be seen at Remington Freeman ltd., New York, NY; the silverware was provided by Yamazaki Tableware Inc., 150 North St., Teterboro, NJ 07608; the china was graciously donated by Fitz and Floyd, Inc., Dallas, Texas.

A FRIEDMAN GROUP BOOK

Copyright © 1992 by Michael Friedman Publishing Group, Inc.

All rights reserved. No part of this publication may be reproduced, stored in a retrieval system, or transmitted, in any form or by any means, electronic, mechanical, photocopying, recording, or otherwise, without the prior written permission of the publisher.

ISBN 0 9627134 3 0

NAPKIN FOLDING
was prepared and produced by
Michael Friedman Publishing Group, Inc.
15 West 26th Street
New York, New York 10010

Editor: Dana Rosen
Art Director: Jeff Batzli
Designer: Lynne Yeamans
Photography Editor: Christopher C. Bain
Illustrator: Steven Arcella
All photographs © Michael Grand, except where noted on page © Tony Cenicola

Typeset by Classic Type, Inc.
Printed in Hong Kong and bound in China by Leefung-Asco Printers Ltd.

CONTENTS

INTRODUCTION

Just as a necktie or scarf adds color and style to an outfit, a decoratively folded napkin really dresses up your table. Napkin folding is fun to do and is appreciated by your guests. It also allows you to be creative by choosing patterns and types of napkins and the kind of fold that will add just the right touch to your meal. Some folded patterns can be real showstoppers, while others add a more subtle note of style to your table. Some designs will make your table look very festive, while others may be very practical, helping you to carry silverware from a buffet table, serving as a placecard holder, keeping a roll warm, hiding an after-dinner mint, or doubling as a hot plate or mitt to protect your hands when passing a hot dish.

Most of the napkin fold patterns here are considered traditional. You may see them adorning the tables of the finest restaurants. Others come from people at home who are creating new ways to decorate their own table. Indeed, you may use the instructions and photographs here to stimulate your own creativity and make your own patterns or variations on those already shown.

TYPES OF NAPKINS

Most designs work best when folded from cloth napkins. If you are using paper napkins, try to use large, three-ply napkins. Many designs require that your napkin be square, so look at the dimensions on the package before purchasing; many paper napkins are not perfectly square. In a pinch, you can always trim a paper napkin to the proper size.

Cloth napkins should be ironed after laundering. Also, many designs will hold their shape better when the napkin has been starched. Ideally, to avoid unwanted creases that may show on the finished design, napkins that have been starched and ironed should be stored perfectly flat until they are used. If this is not possible, then you can either re-iron them before using, or plan ahead by folding the beginning creases for the design you think you may use next (such as folded in half, thirds, or quarters), and storing them in this shape.

Cloth napkins made from polyester blend will tend to resist creases more than all-cotton or linen napkins, and may even begin to unfold themselves. Use these napkins for folds that are anchored in a glass or napkin ring, where the "spreading" effect may be desirable. Avoid using them for designs that stand on their own and require sturdy material.

SIZE OF NAPKINS

While most designs work best when folded from a large napkin (around twenty inches [51 cm] square), more intricate folds may require an even larger napkin, while simpler folds may be possible from small napkins. Experiment with what you have on hand to see what works best.

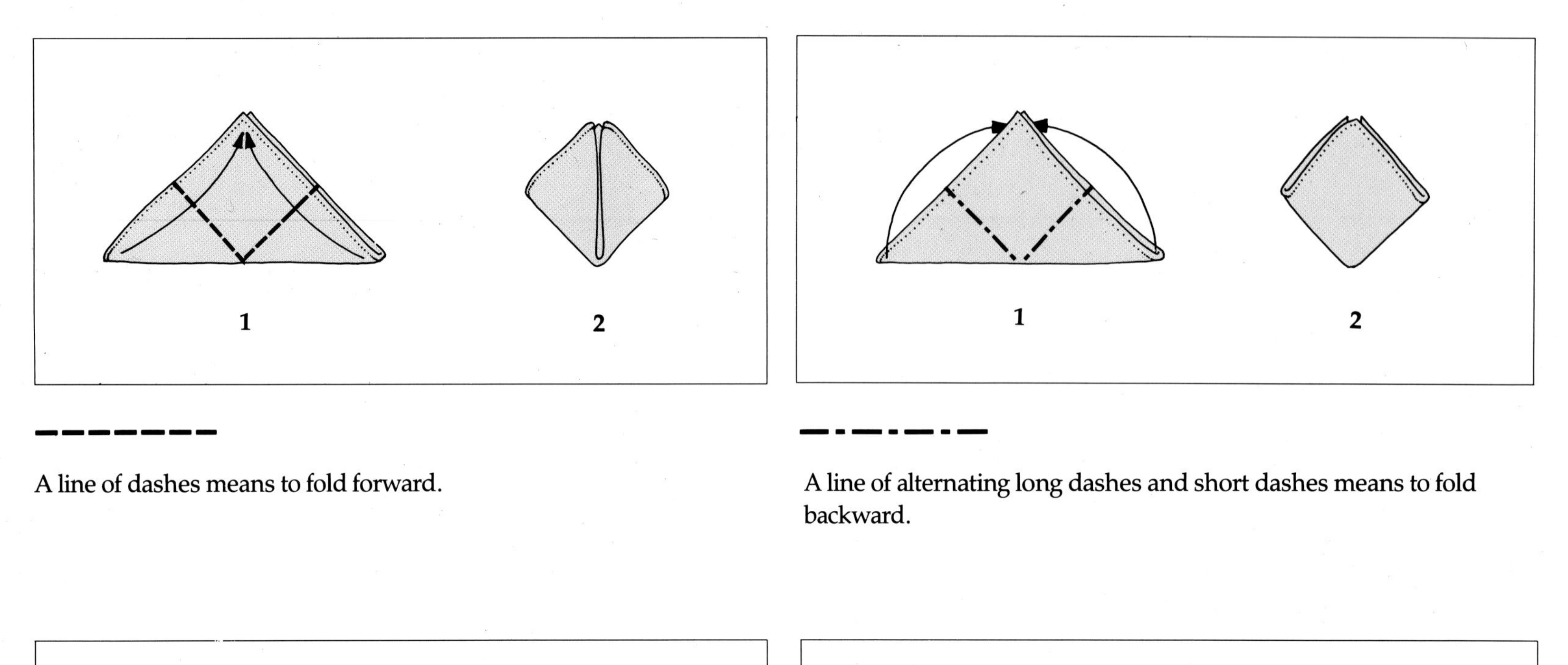

A line of dashes means to fold forward.

A line of alternating long dashes and short dashes means to fold backward.

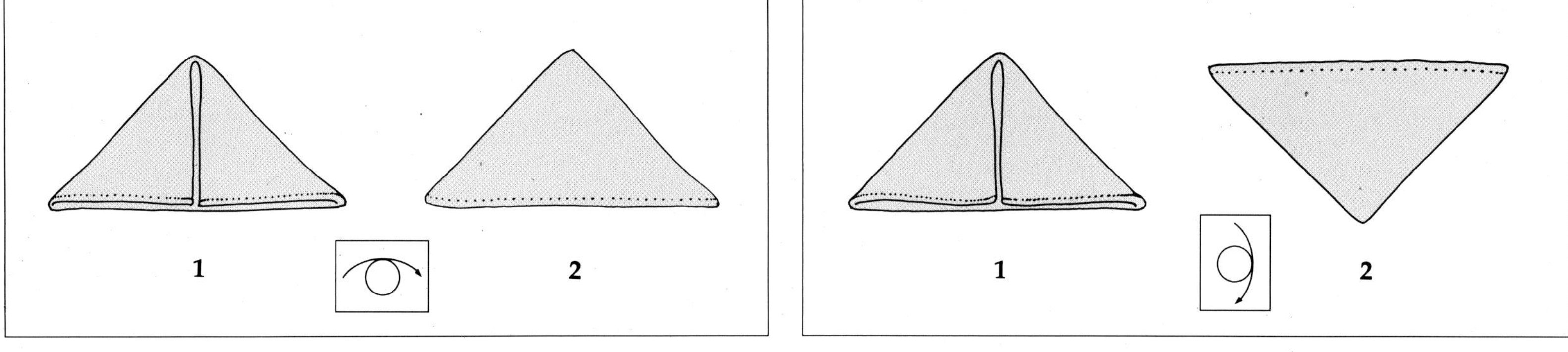

A looped arrow means to turn the model over in the direction of the arrow.

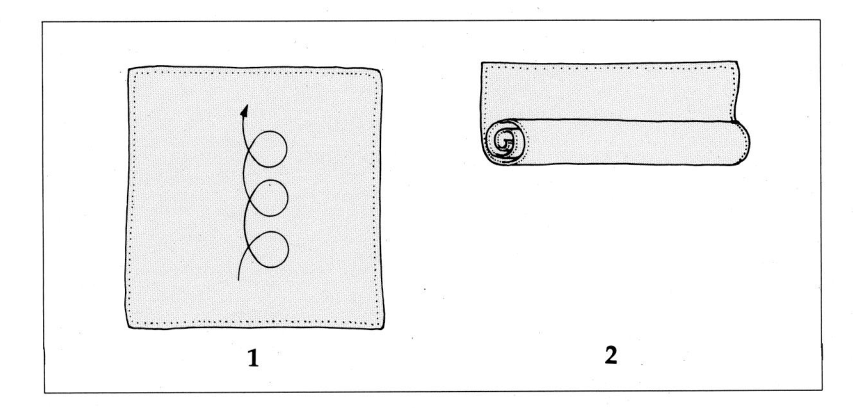

An arrow with many loops means to roll the napkin in the direction of the arrow.

A dotted line indicates a hidden edge, or the position of a fold after it is made.

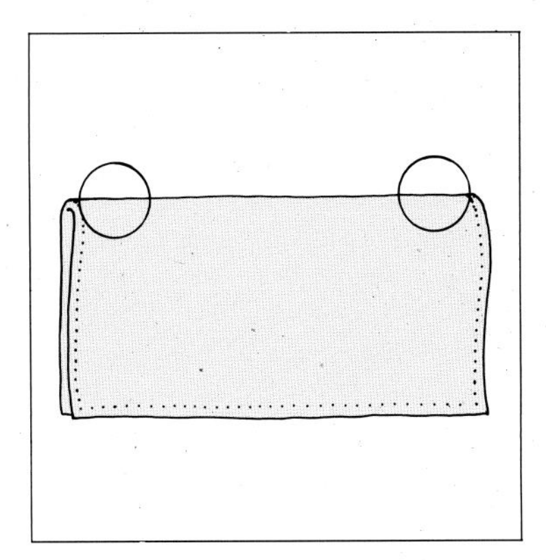

A circle means to hold the napkin here.

HOW TO FOLD A NAPKIN INTO QUARTERS

Some of the directions in this book instruct you to begin with a napkin folded into quarters. If you are using a paper napkin, this is exactly how it usually comes in the package and you are ready to begin. Otherwise, here are directions for folding into quarters:

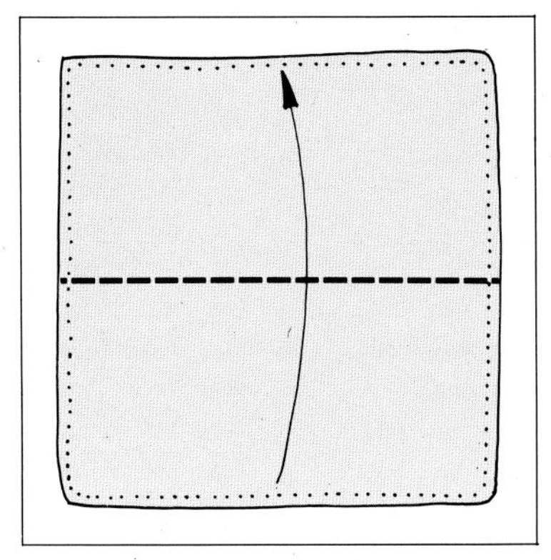

1. Fold the napkin in half.

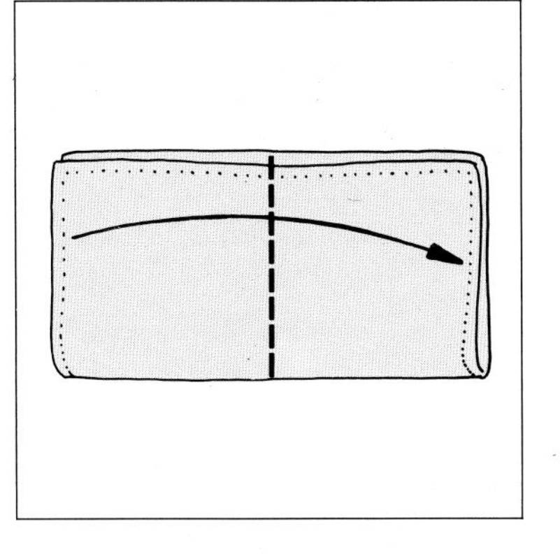

2. Fold in half again.

Four loose corners

3. Your napkin is now folded into quarters. One corner will have four loose corners. The beginning instruction for the fold will usually tell you where to place this corner.

CHAPTER ONE

Flat Designs

BUN WARMER

(Adapted by the author)

Here's a novel way to present your napkins and keep each guest's bun or roll warm and fresh. Use a large cloth napkin (approximately twenty inches [51 cm]).

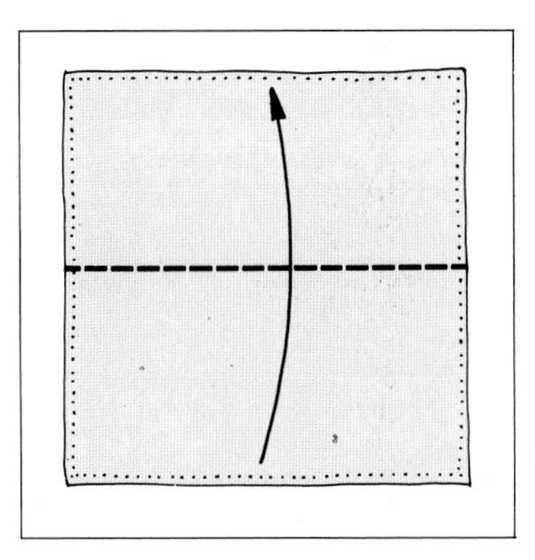

1. Begin with an open, square napkin. Fold the bottom edge up to the top edge.

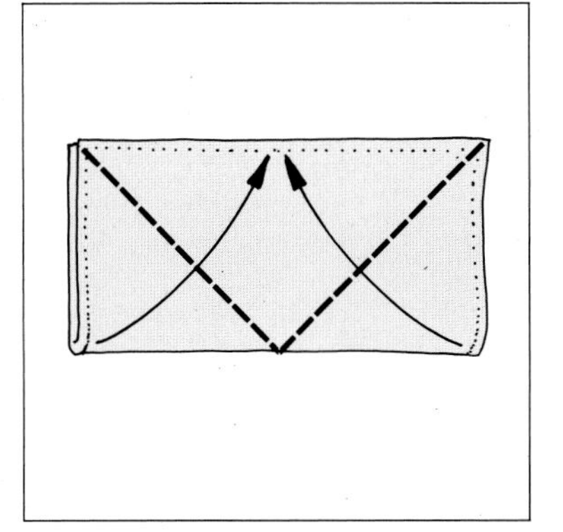

2. Bring the right and left bottom points up to meet at the center of the top edge.

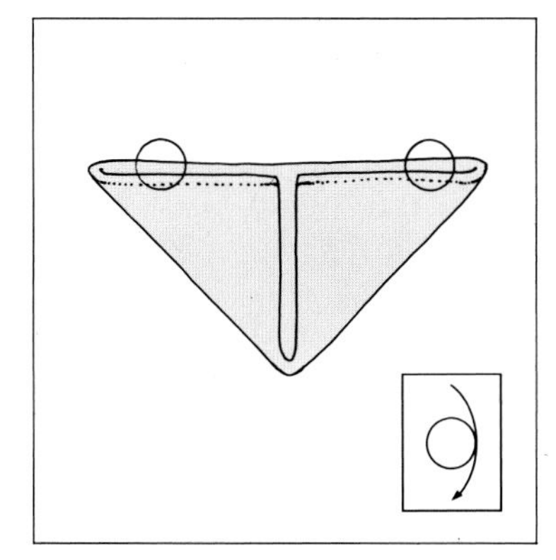

3. Hold the top edge of the triangle (the long edge) by the side points and flip the napkin over to the other side, so that the long edge of the triangle is now at the bottom.

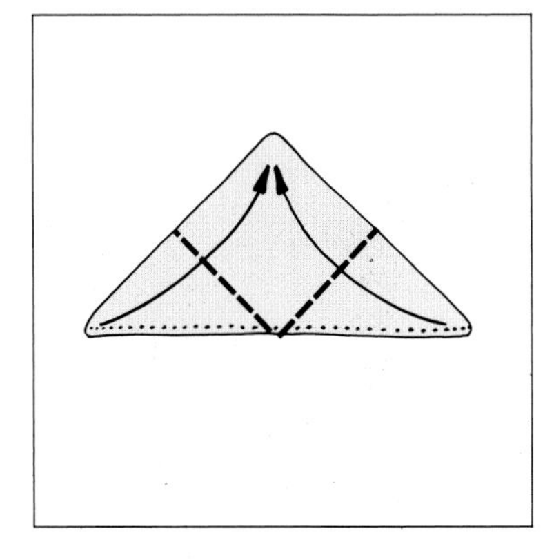

4. Bring the side points up to the top point.

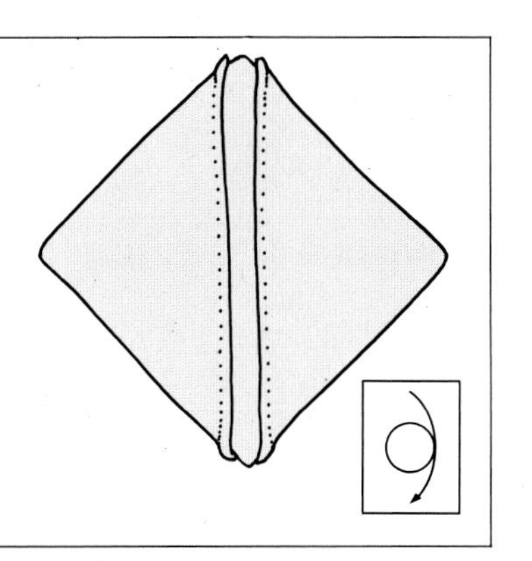

5. Hold the top points and flip the napkin over again. (The top corner will now be at the bottom.)

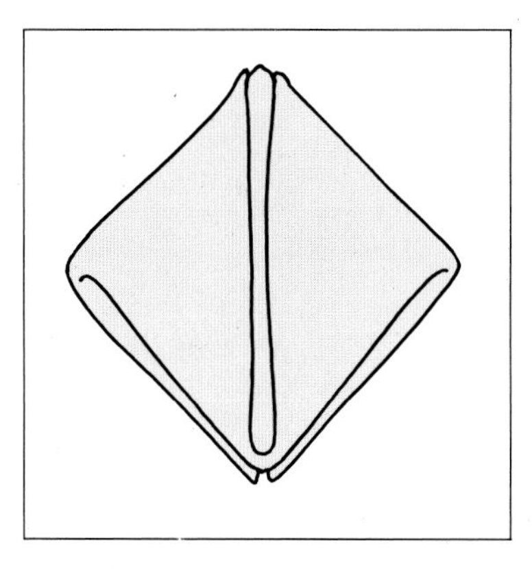

6. Completed Bun Warmer. Slip a bun into the pocket formed by the center slit or lift up the first point at the bottom corner and hide the bun under this layer.

DIAGONAL STRIPES

The very elegant look of this design adds a touch of class to your table. If you wish, silverware, a flower, or a name card can be inserted into the pockets behind the bands.

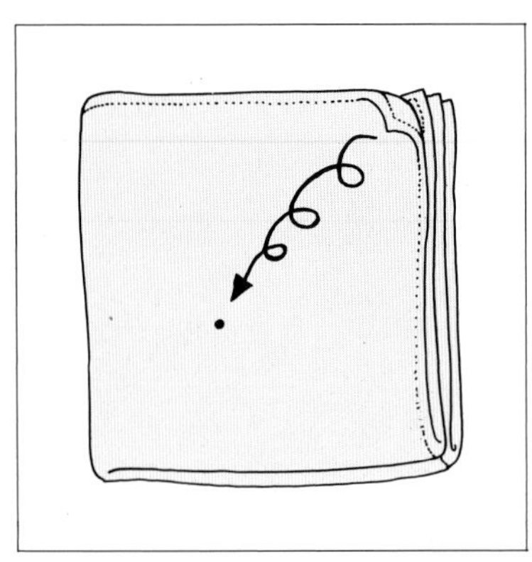

1. Begin with a napkin folded into quarters. Position the napkin so that the four free corners are at the top right. Lift the first free corner and roll it diagonally down toward the opposite corner, stopping just past midway or as far as you can comfortably roll. Flatten the roll into a narrow band.

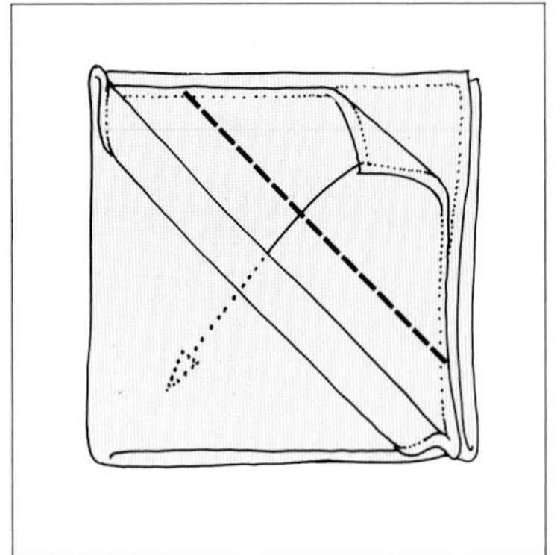

2. Lift the band slightly and at the same time lift the next free corner at the top right. Slip the corner part way into the pocket behind the band. The folded edge should form a band that is parallel to and approximately the same width as the first band.

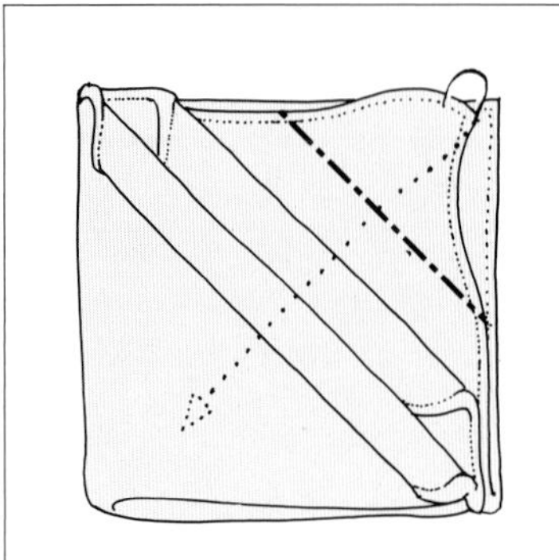

3. Lift the third free corner and fold it backward and behind the second band to form a third band equal in width to the first two.

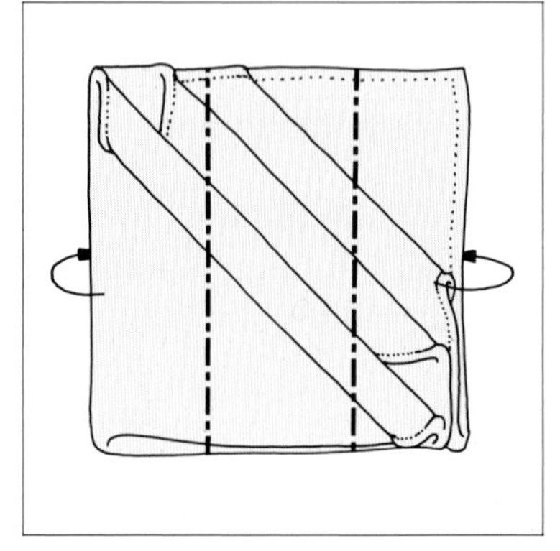

4. Fold the right and left sides to the back.

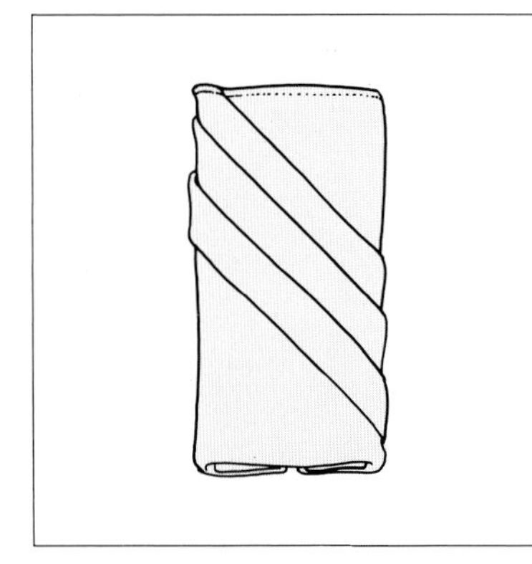

5. Completed Diagonal Stripes.

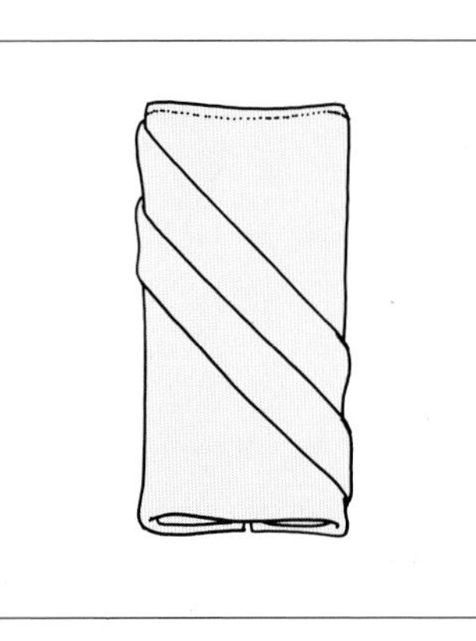

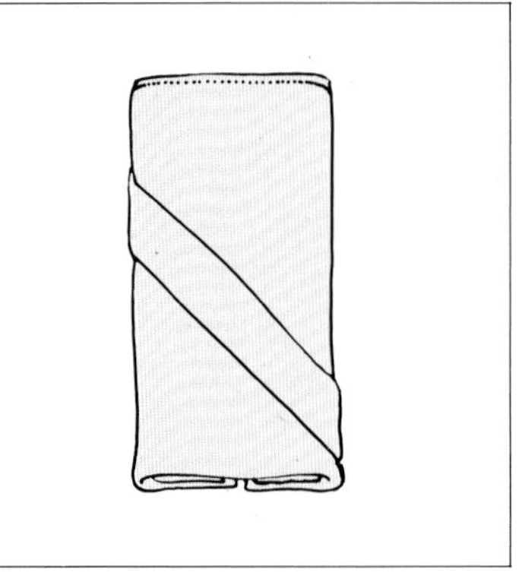

Variation: Instead of forming three bands, this fold can be made with either one or two bands.

© Tony Cenicola

DIAMOND IN THE SQUARE

(Contributed by Susan Kalish)

For a bold geometric effect, choose a cloth napkin in a color that contrasts with the color of your dinnerware.

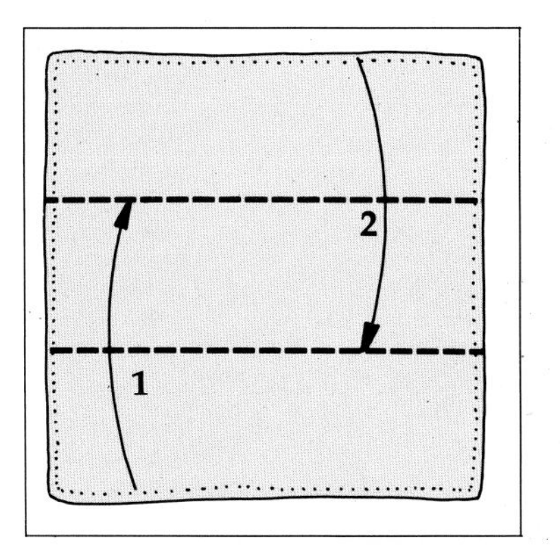

1. Begin with an open, square napkin. Fold it in thirds (as you would fold a letter). The open edge should be at the bottom.

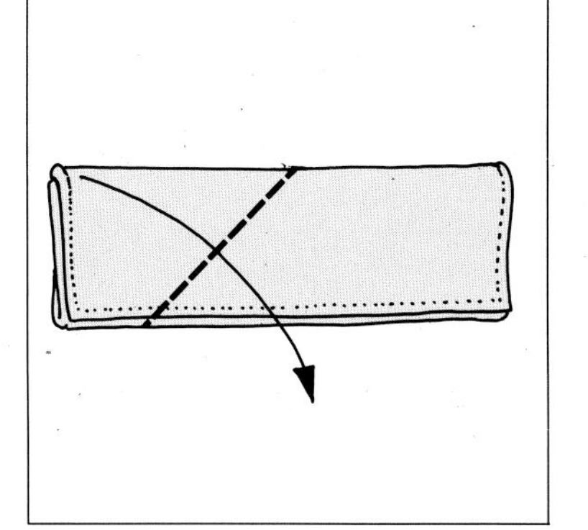

2. Place a finger at the center of the top edge and bring the top left corner down.

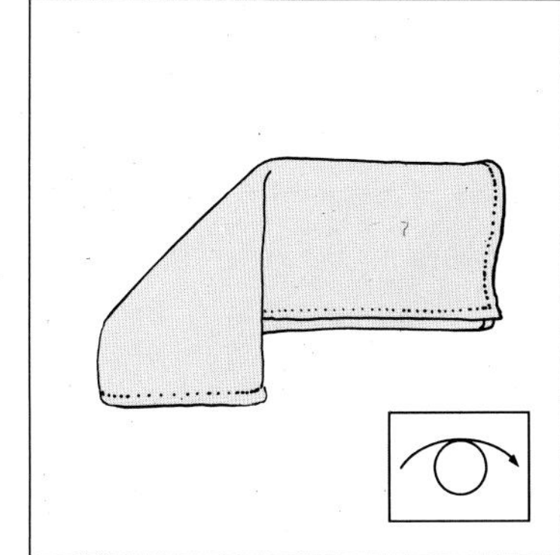

3. Turn the napkin over and position it so that the slanted edge is on the right.

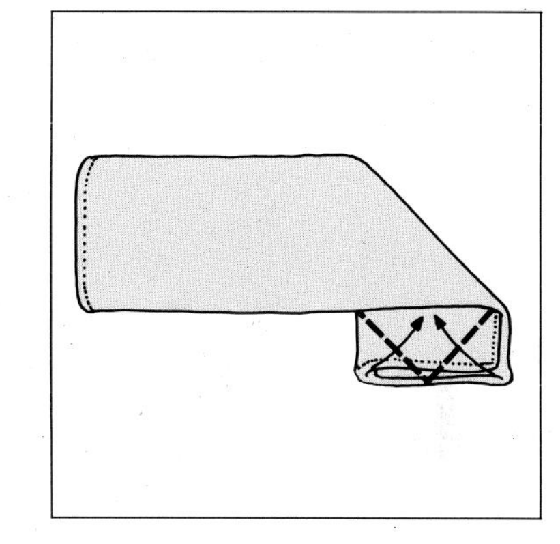

4. A rectangle should extend below the bottom of the right side. Fold the right and left corners of the rectangle up to the folded edge.

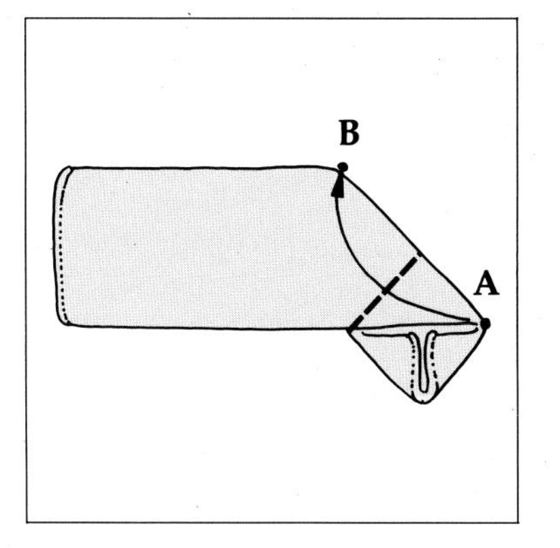

5. Fold point A up to lie on point B, creating a diamond shape at one end of the strip.

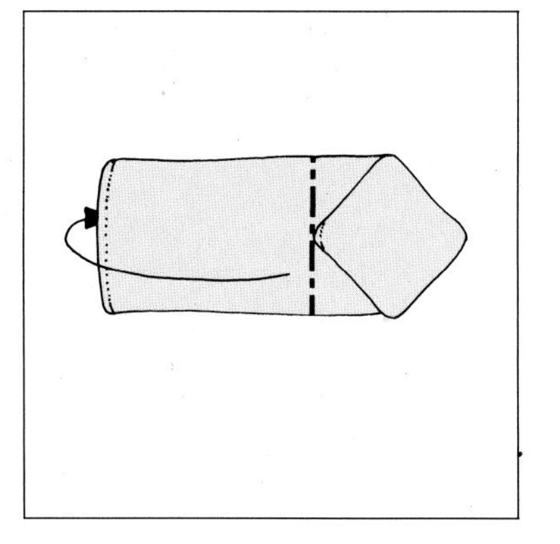

6. Fold the left edge of the strip backward so that the edge lies directly behind the right corner of the diamond.

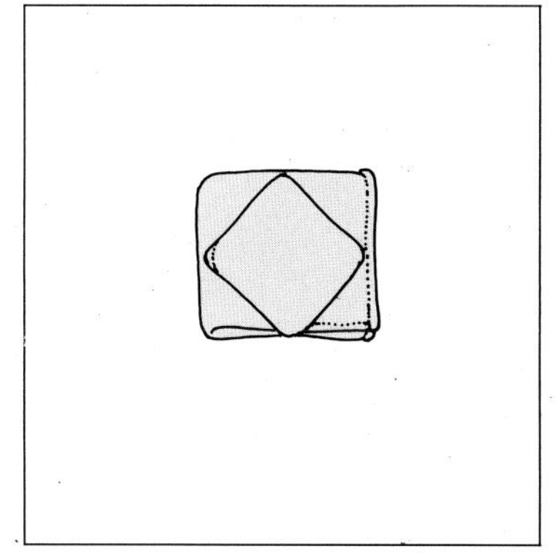

7. Completed Diamond in the Square.

DOUBLE FLAP PURSE

(Design by the author)

This handsome fold looks distinguished draped across a plate with the flaps pointing down, like a purse, or turned sideways and placed to the left of the plate.

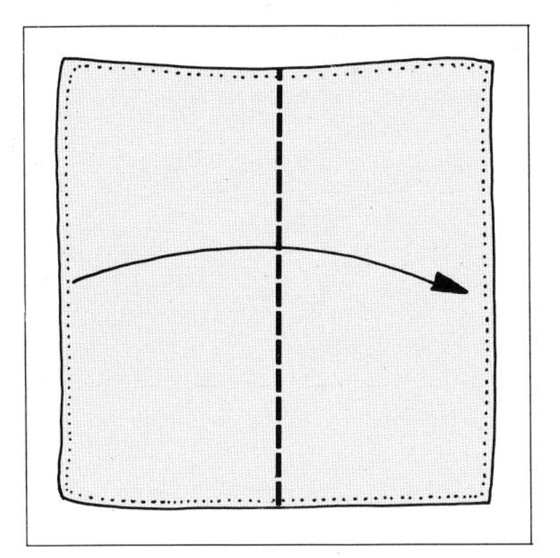

1. Begin with an open, square napkin. Fold the left side over to the right.

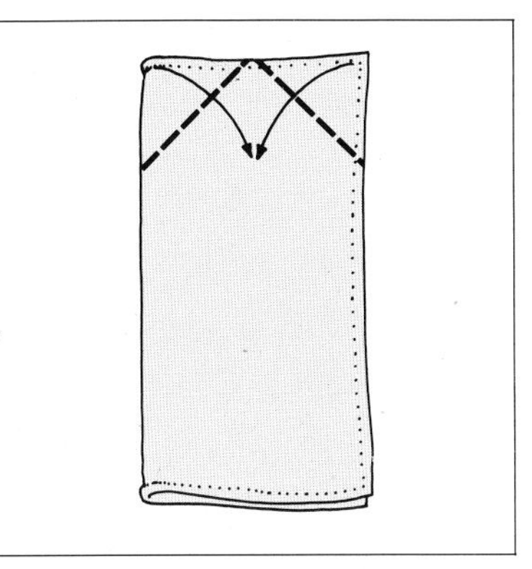

2. Fold the top corners down to form a point at the top.

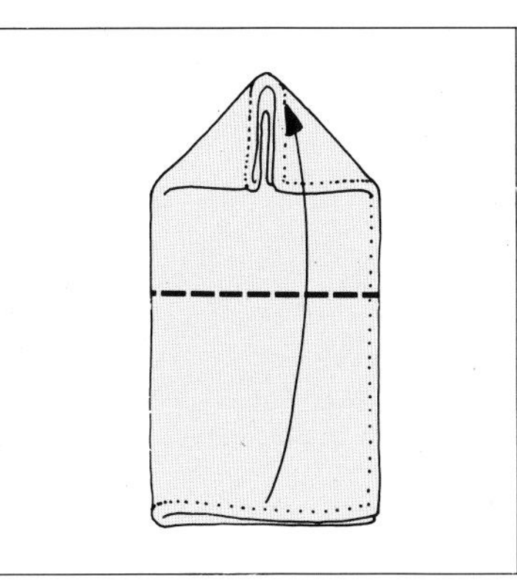

3. Fold the bottom edge up so it covers the top point.

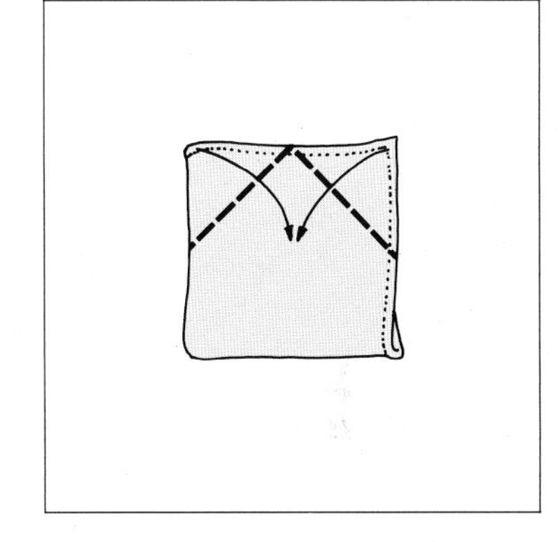

4. Fold the new top corners down to form another point that lies over the point made in step 2.

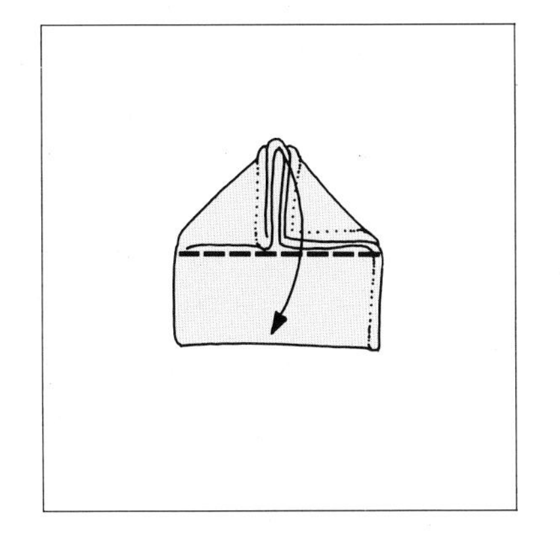

5. Fold the front point down to the bottom edge of the napkin.

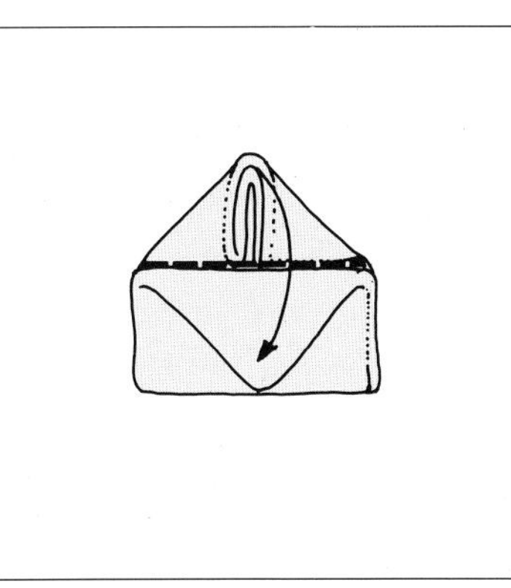

6. Fold the remaining point down so that it rests slightly higher than the first.

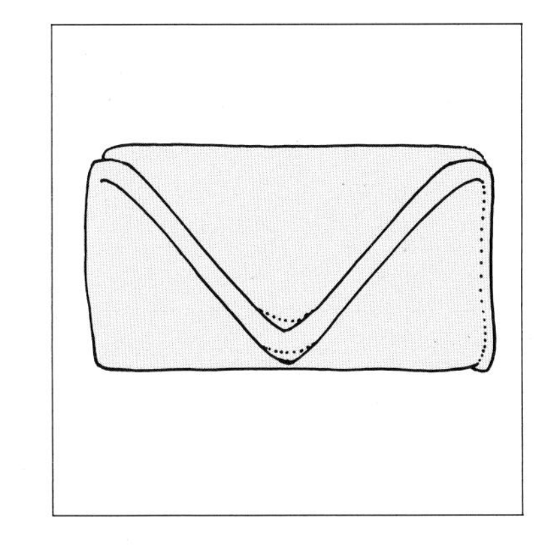

7. Completed Double Flap Purse.

EMPEROR'S ROBE

(Design by the author)

This regal design looks best using a cloth napkin at least twenty inches (51 cm) square.

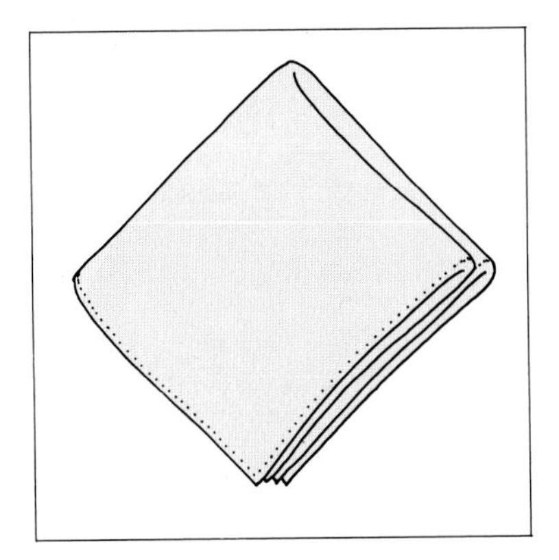

1. Fold the napkin into quarters. Place it on the table so that the four free corners are at the bottom.

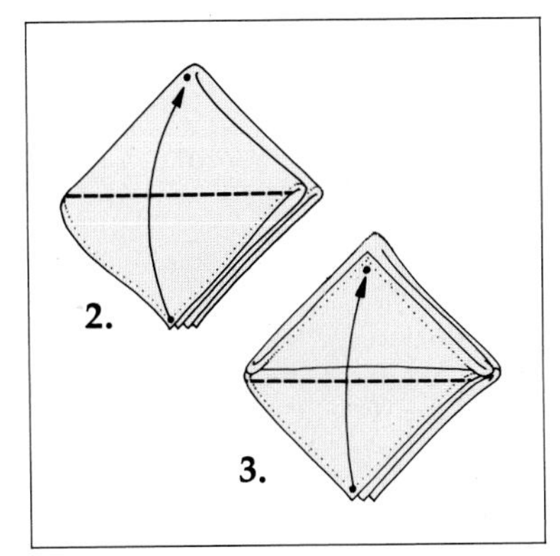

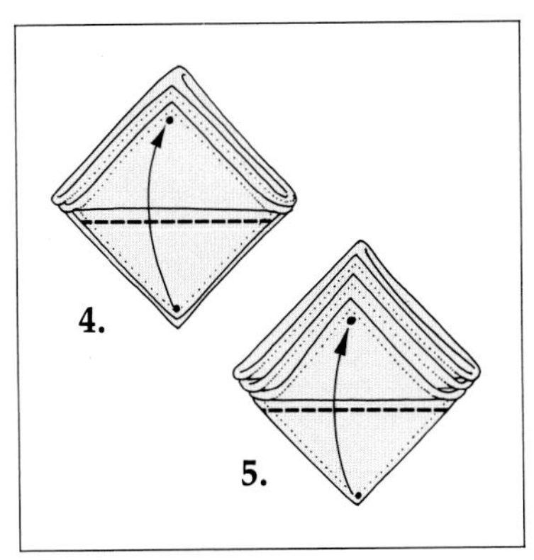

2–5. Fold up each of the bottom corners in succession, bringing each a little lower than the previous corner.

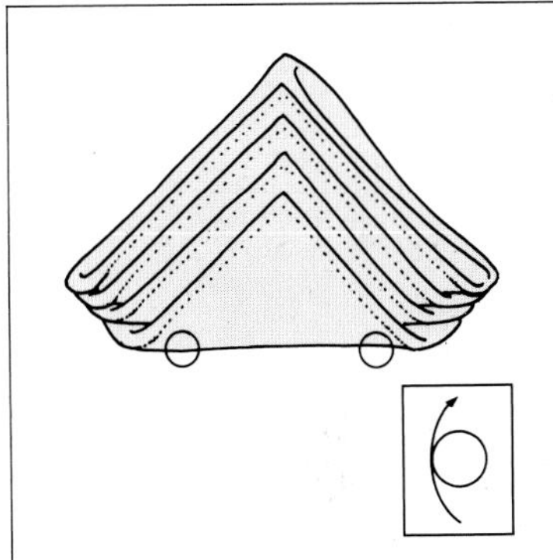

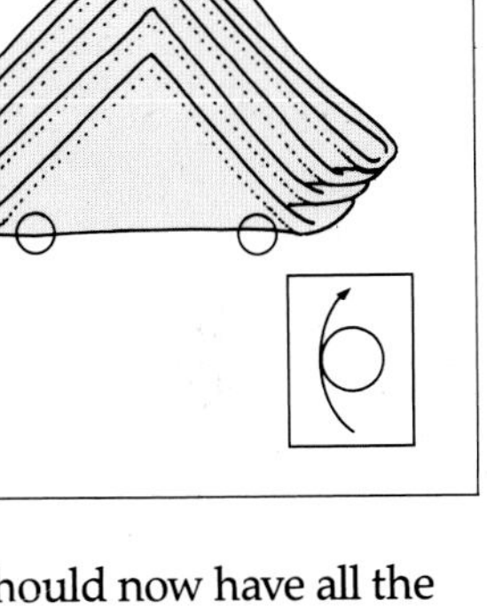

6. You should now have all the corners folded up and evenly spaced apart. Hold the napkin at the bottom edge and flip it over so that the bottom edge is now at the top.

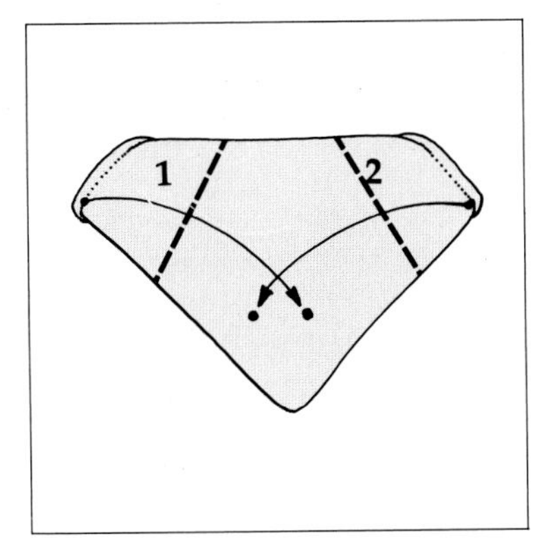

7. Fold the side corners toward the center as shown (see drawing 8).

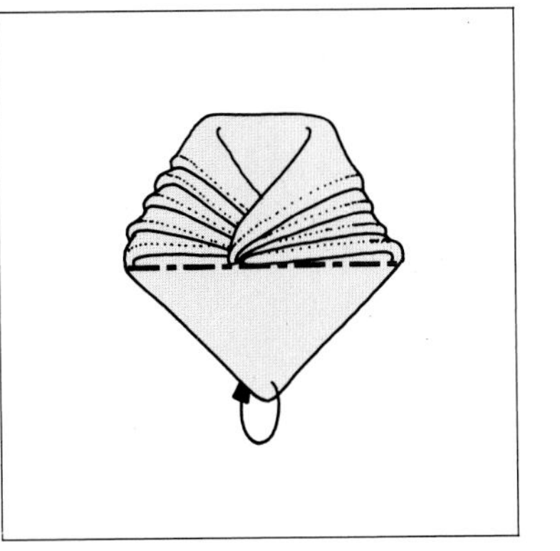

8. Fold the bottom point behind.

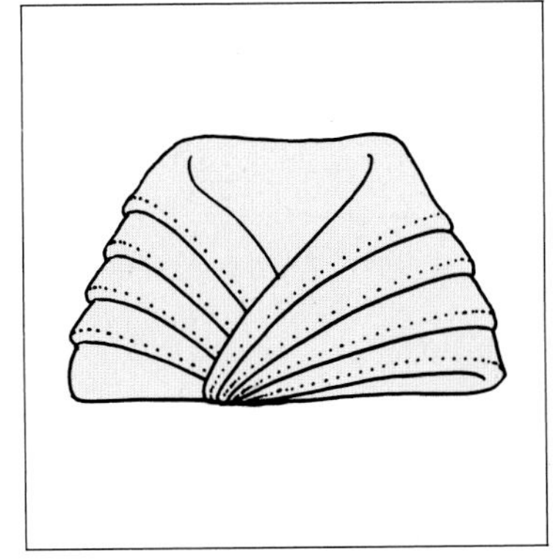

9. Completed Emperor's Robe.

MONOGRAM FOLD

(Contributed by Susan Kalish)

This fold is an ideal way to show off a napkin with a monogram, a decoration, or a lacy edge at one corner.

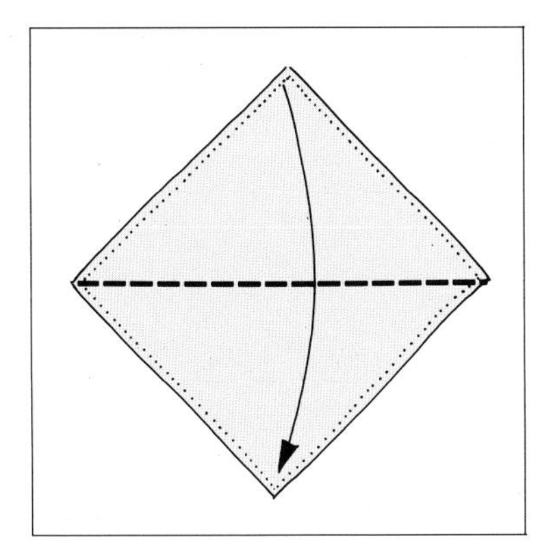

1. Begin with an open, square napkin in the shape of a diamond. The corner with the monogram or decoration should be at the bottom, on the underside of the napkin. Bring the top corner down to the bottom corner.

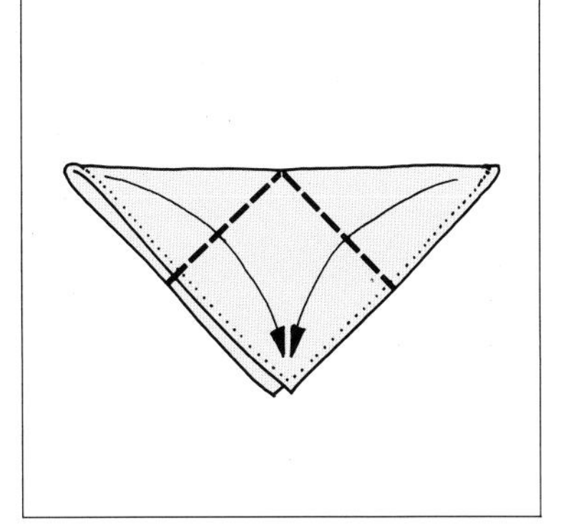

2. Fold the side corners down to the bottom point.

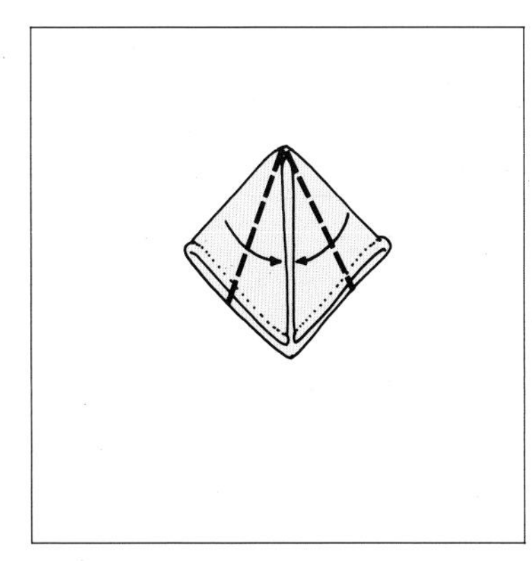

3. Fold the side edges that connect at the top corner inward to meet at the center.

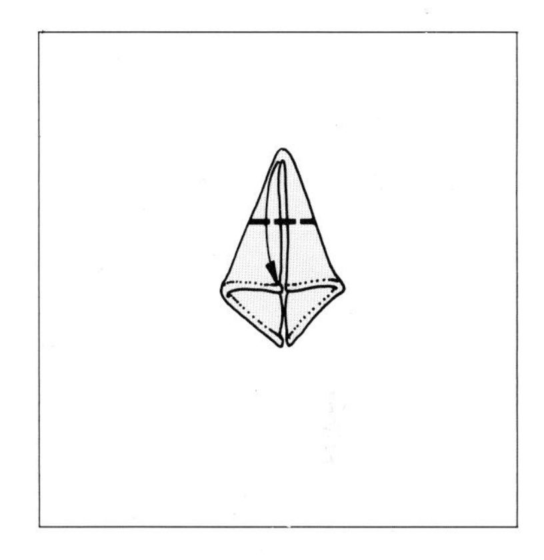

4. Fold the top point down to meet the corners that you folded in the last step.

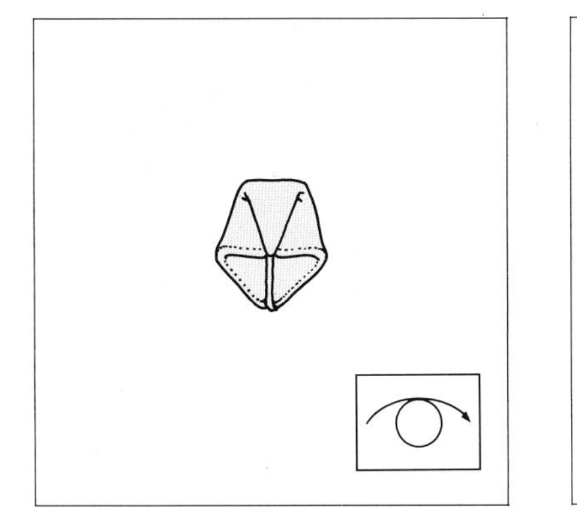

5. Turn the napkin over.

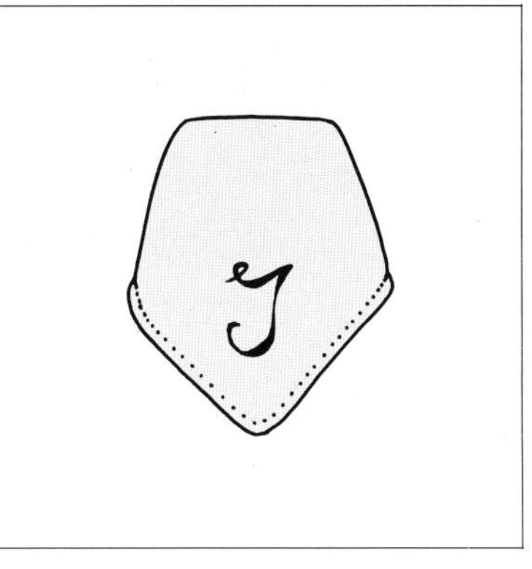

6. Completed Monogram fold.

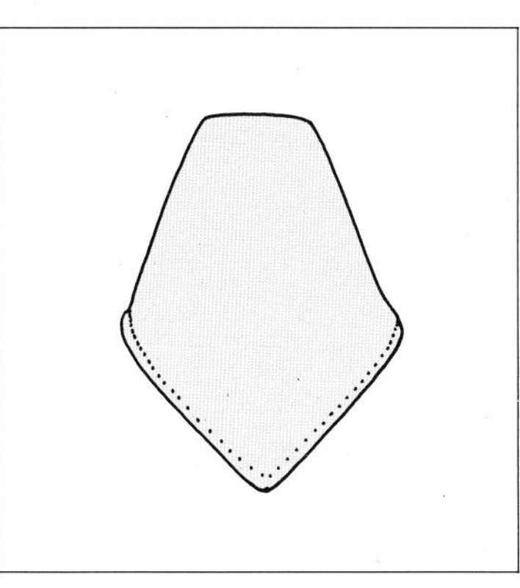

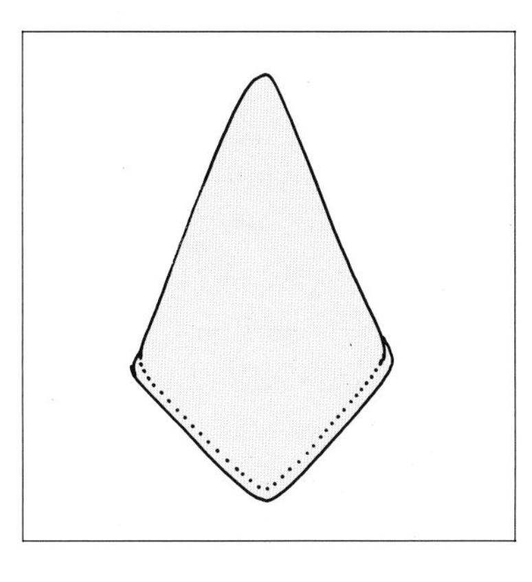

Variation: At step 4, bring the top point down only slightly or not at all. This will give the napkin a longer shape, more suitable for placement at the side of a plate or under a fork.

POINTED POCKET

The tall, slender shape and deep pocket of this design make it a suitable holder for a flower, breadsticks, straws, chopsticks, or silverware.

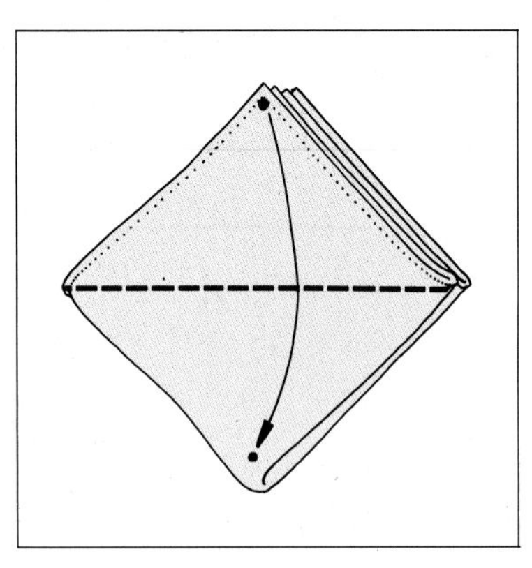

1. Begin with a napkin folded in quarters. Place it on the table so that the four free corners are at the top. Bring the top corner of the first layer down to a little above the bottom corner.

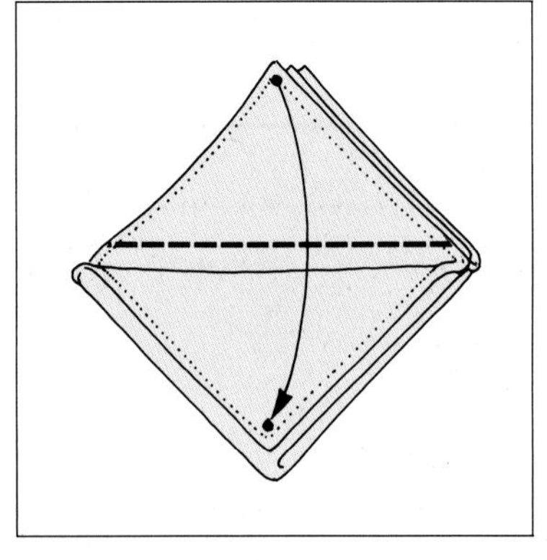

2. Bring the second layer down so that the corner lies a little above the corner of the first layer folded down.

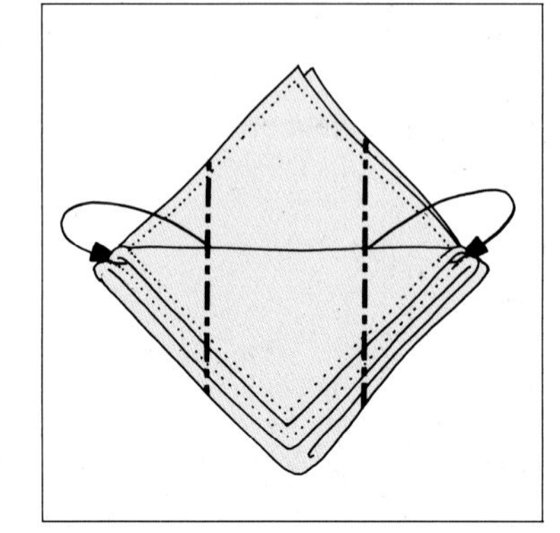

3. Fold the side corners behind to overlap at the back of the napkin. (You may wish to turn the napkin over to make this step easier.)

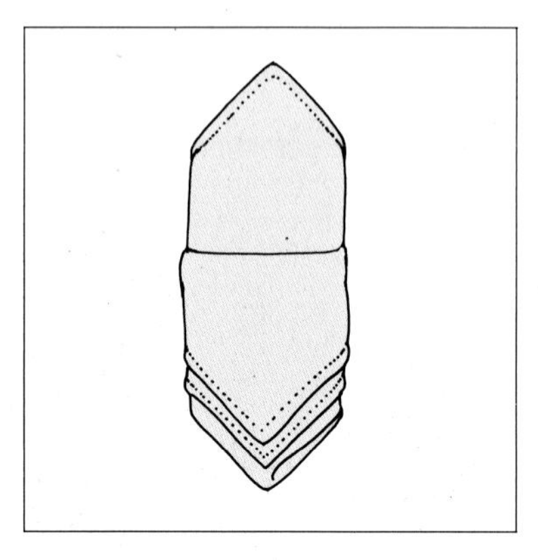

4. Completed Pointed Pocket.

SILK PURSE

Add an elegant touch to your table with this beautiful Silk Purse design. Use a large cloth napkin.

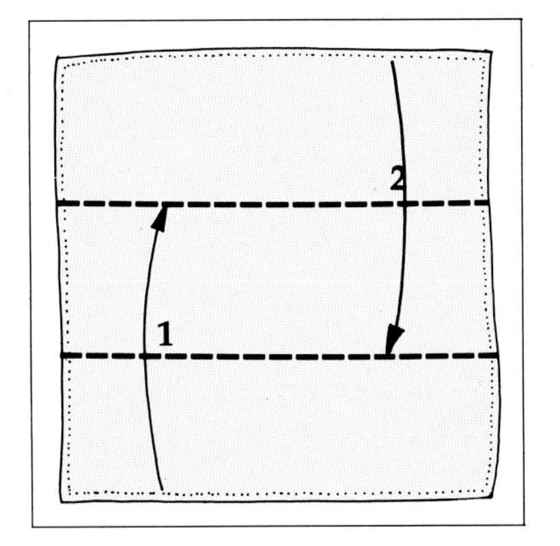

1. Begin with an open, square napkin. Fold the napkin in thirds (as you would fold a letter) so that the open edge is on the bottom.

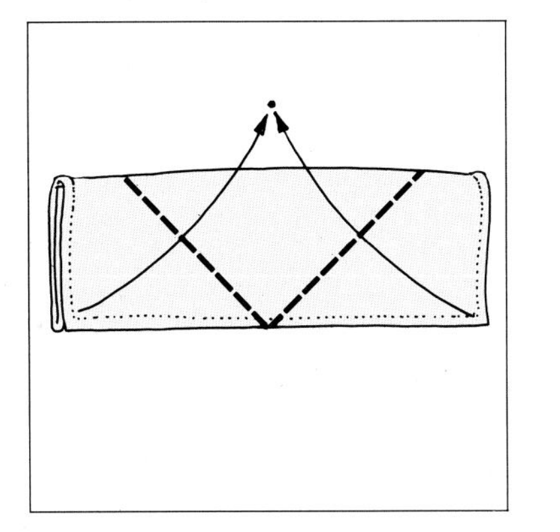

2. Place a finger at the center of the bottom edge and fold up the right and left bottom corners so that both sides of the bottom edge meet at the center.

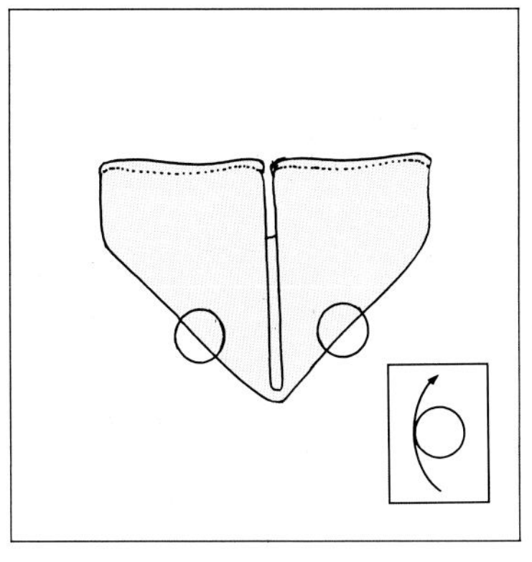

3. Hold the slanted edges of the napkin and flip it over to the other side.

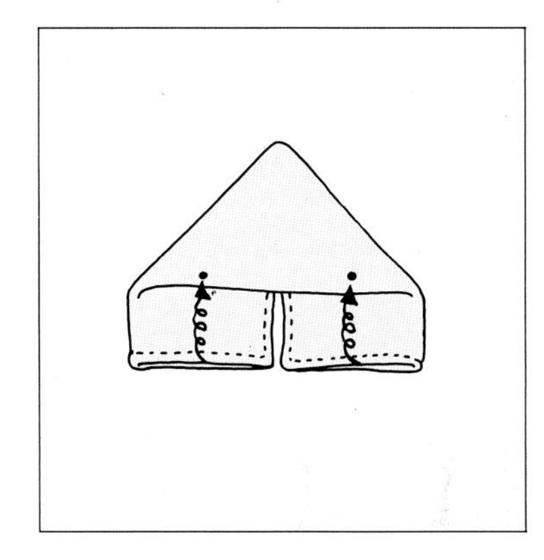

4. Two rectangles extend below the base of a large triangle. Tightly roll each rectangle up as far as you can (just past the base of the triangle).

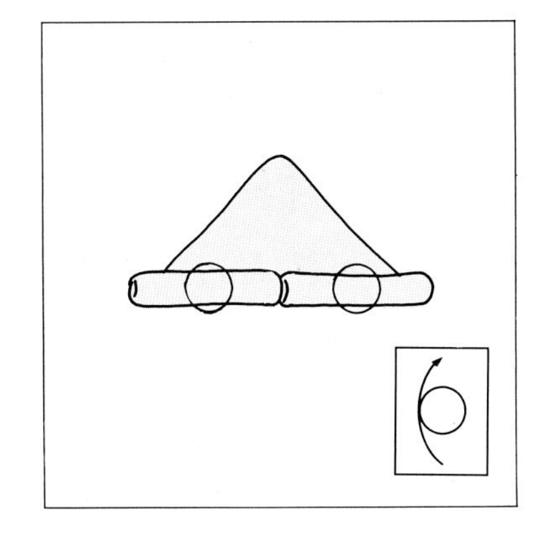

5. While holding the rolls tightly in both hands, flip the napkin over to the other side.

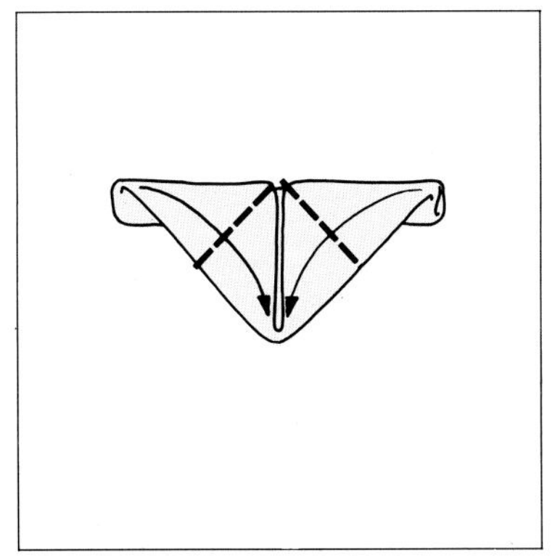

6. Bring the top side corners of the triangle down to the bottom corner.

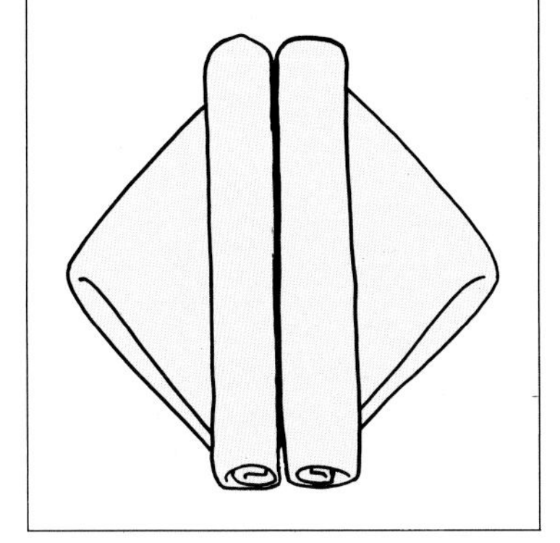

7. Completed Silk Purse Tighten the rolls if necessary.

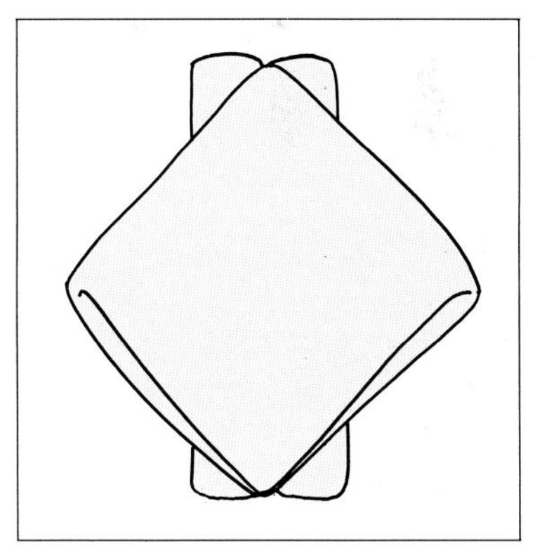

Variation: Turn the napkin over after the last step and the design will resemble a mortarboard, an appropriate design for a graduation party.

SLENDER POINTS

This is a fairly simple and versatile fold that can be placed on or beside a plate, in a glass, or slipped through a napkin ring.

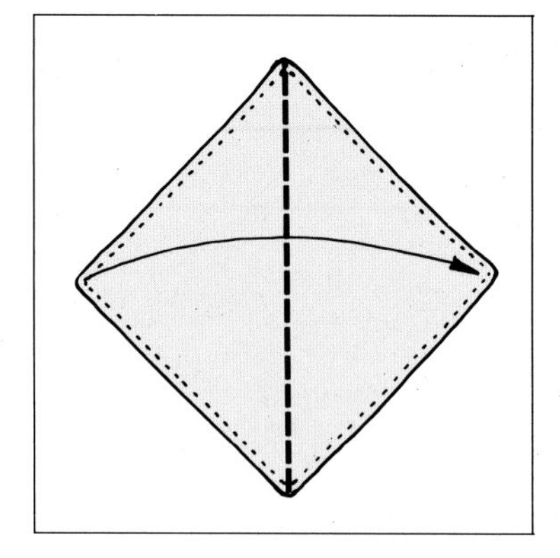

1. Begin with an open, square napkin, turned so that it is shaped like a diamond. Bring the left side corner over to the right side corner.

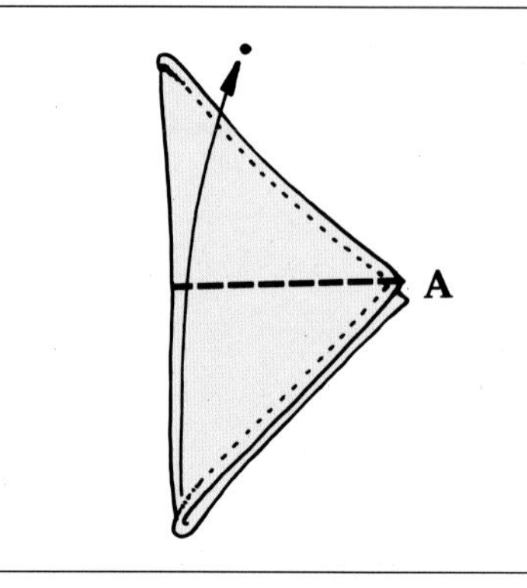

2. Place one finger at the right side corner (A) and lift the bottom point up on a fold that begins at corner A. Place the bottom point slightly to the right of the top point.

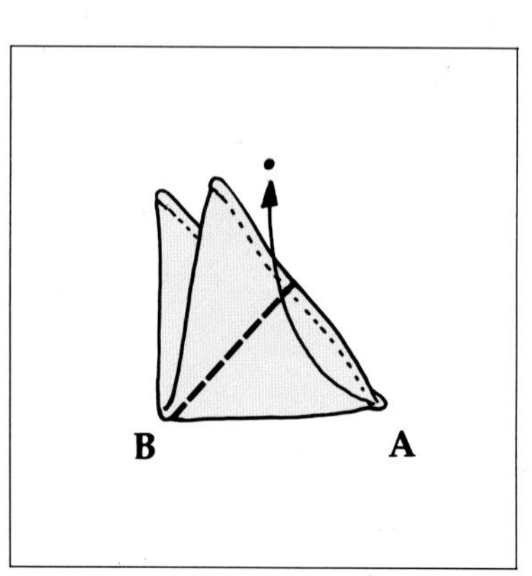

3. Place a finger at the bottom left corner (B) and lift the bottom right point up on a fold that begins at corner B. Place point A slightly to the right of the other two top points.

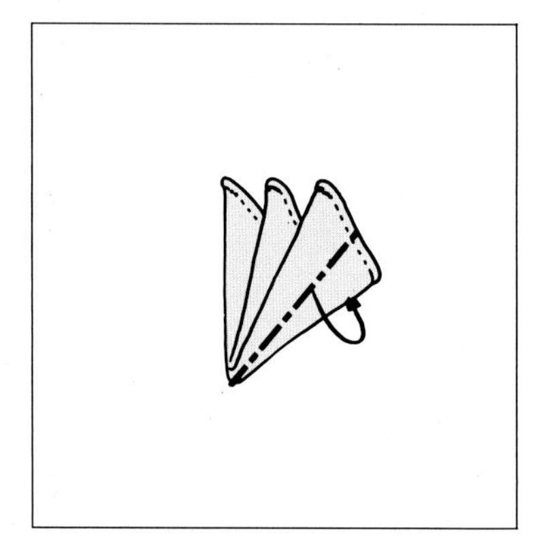

4. Fold the bottom right side backward to give the napkin a more slender form.

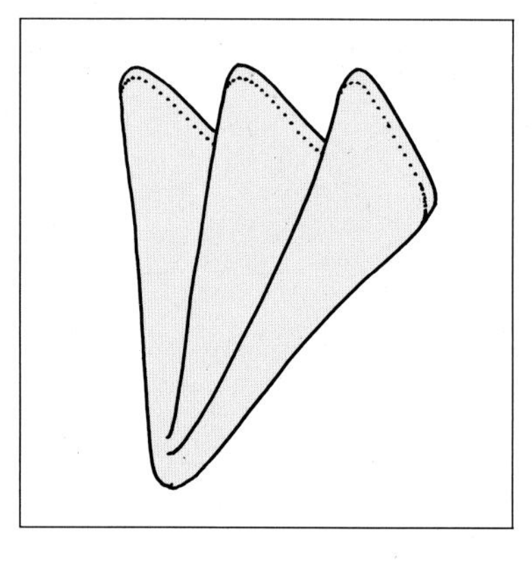

5. Completed Slender Points. If you wish to place this fold in a glass, tuck the bottom point under before inserting.

TRI-FOLD

This design will add elegance to a formal dinner without overpowering the traditional dinnerware or other table decor. If you are using name cards, place the Tri-Fold horizontally on each plate and slip the card behind one of the folded edges. For an extra-special occasion, prepare menu cards listing what will be served and slip them behind the other folded edge.

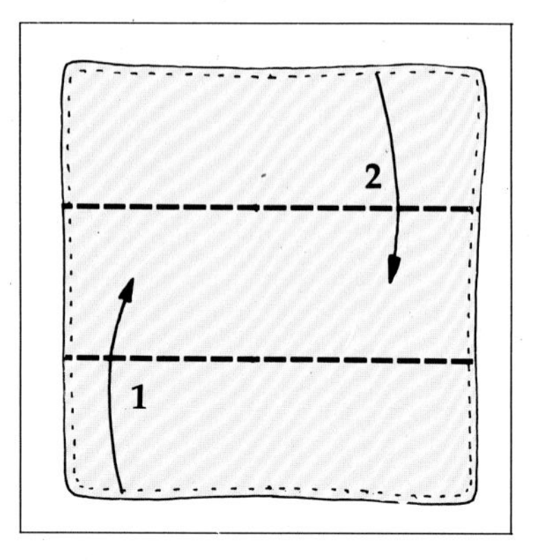

1. Begin with an open napkin. Fold the napkin in thirds, as shown.

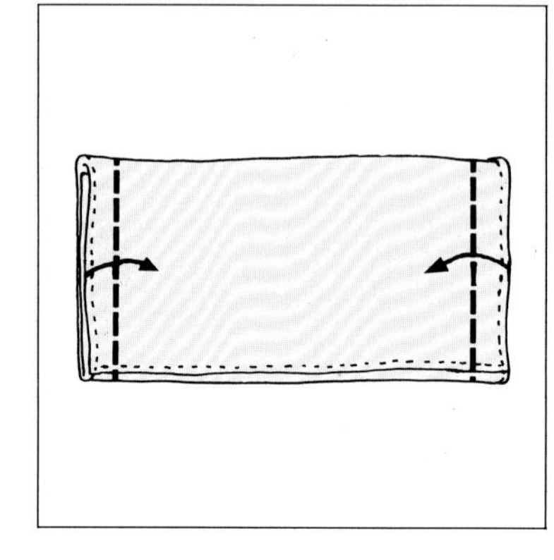

2. Fold in the right and left sides to form a border on each side (approximately two inches [5 cm]) wide.

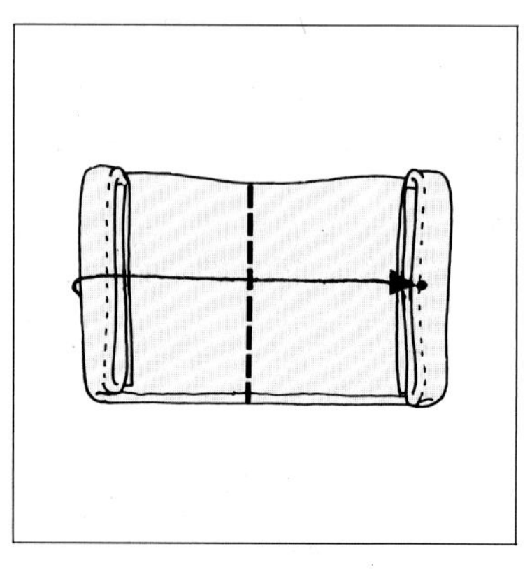

3. Bring the left side over to cover the open edges of the right border.

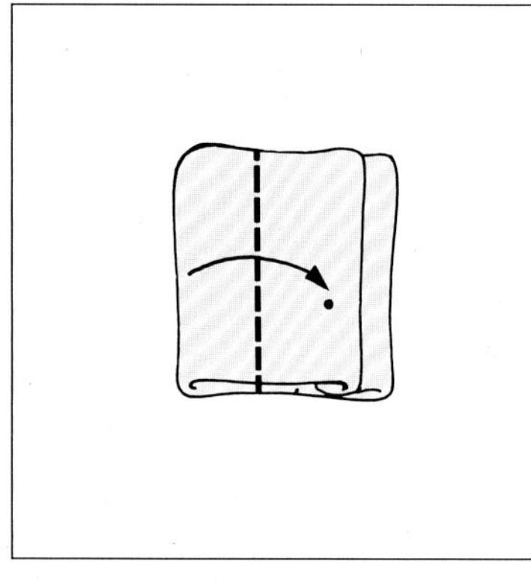

4. Bring the left side toward the right so that each of the folded edges on the right are the same distance apart (see drawing 5).

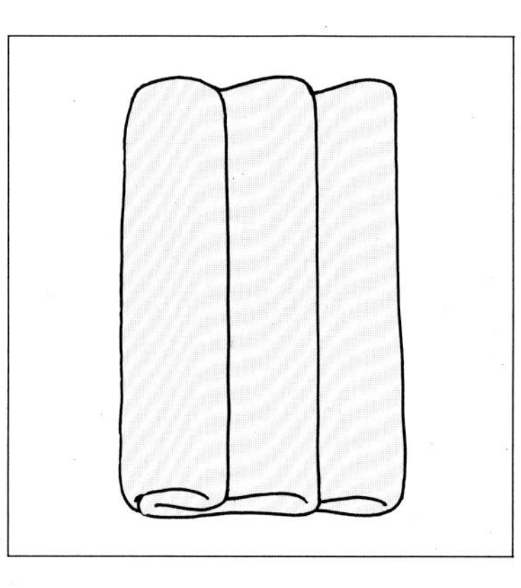

5. The completed Tri-Fold can be placed in a horizontal or vertical position.

Menu
Antipasto
Michael

CHAPTER TWO

Sculptured Designs

BUTTERFLY

(Design by the author)

Invite spring to your table with this decorative Butterfly design.

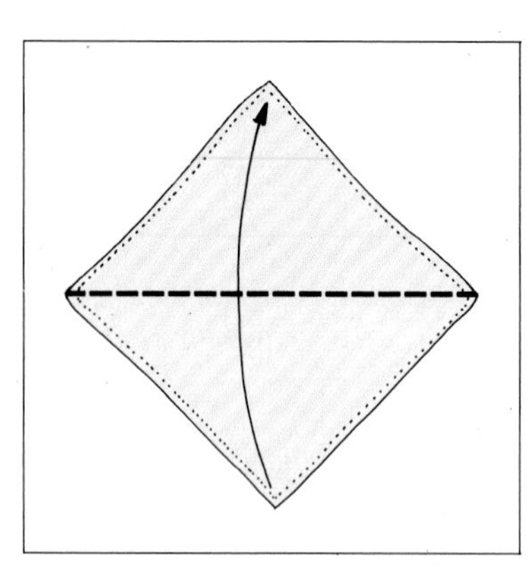

1. Begin with an open, square napkin in the shape of a diamond. Bring the bottom corner up to the top corner.

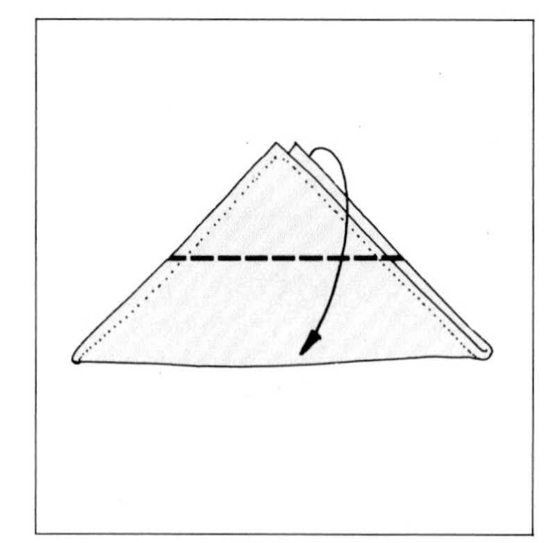

2. Bring the top points down to the center of the bottom edge.

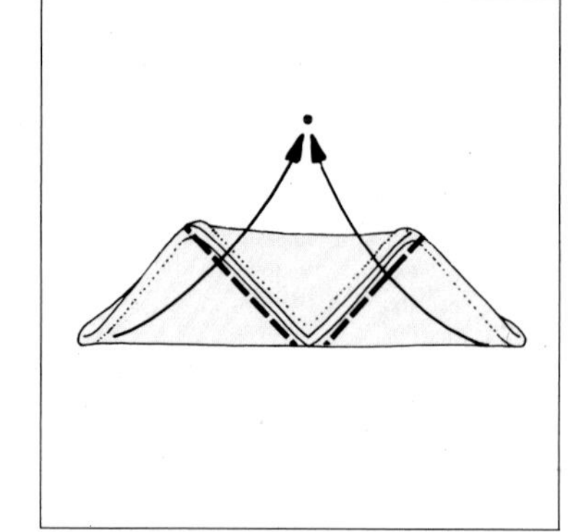

3. Fold both side points up.

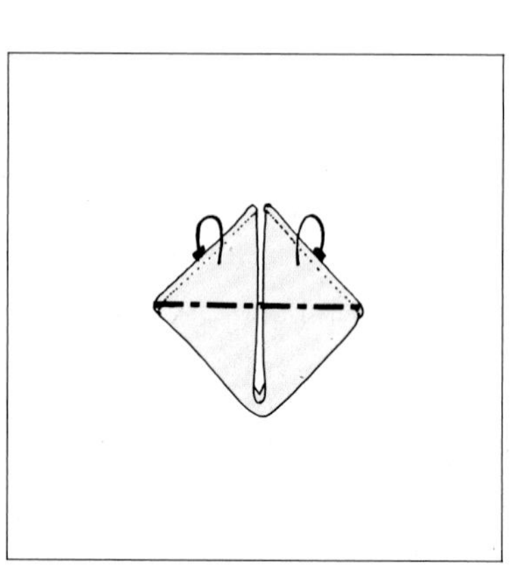

4. Fold the top half of each triangle backward to wrap behind the horizontal folded edge.

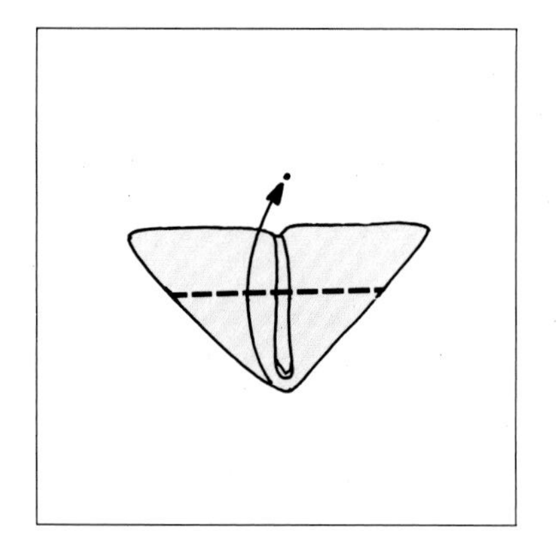

5. Lift up the middle bottom point and position it slightly above the top of the triangle (see drawing 6).

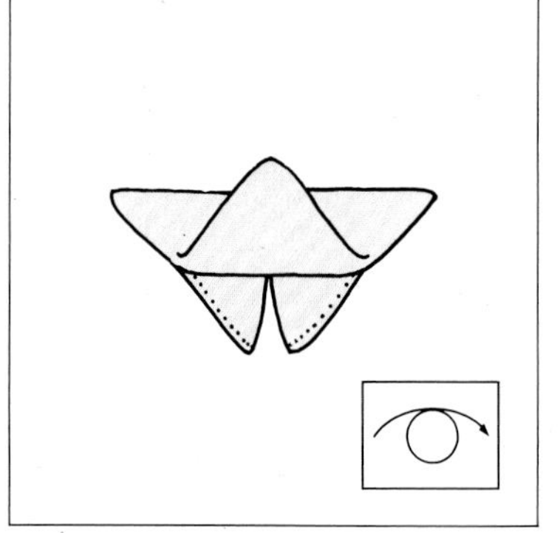

6. Turn the napkin over.

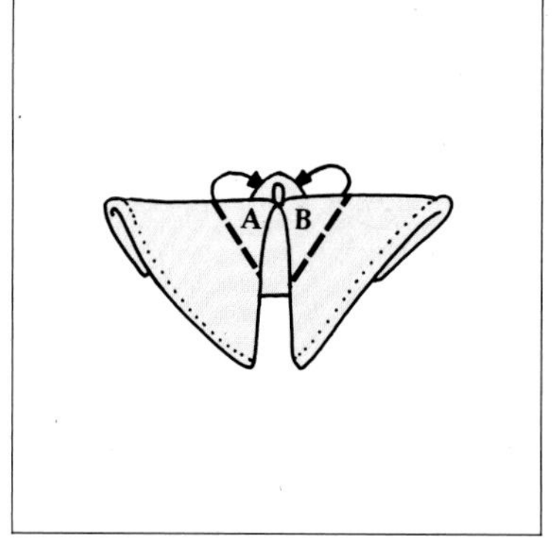

7. Hold the napkin at A and B and push your hands together. The center of the napkin (the body of the butterfly) should raise up and the wings should shift to the position shown in drawing 8.

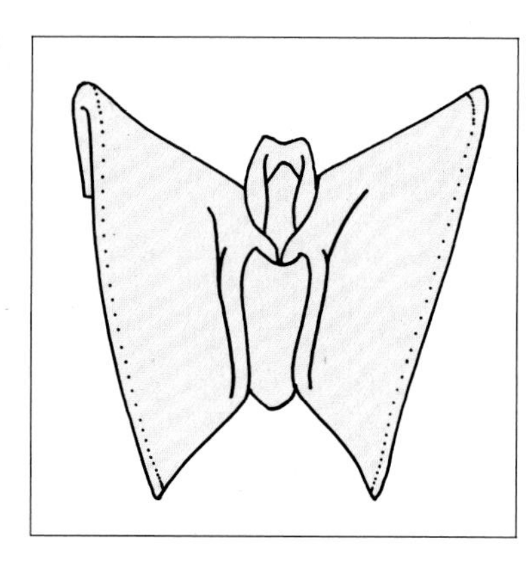

8. Completed Butterfly. If you are using a paper napkin, fold the body over to the right and then to the left to sharpen the creases that separate the body from the wings.

CROWN

The Crown is a classic napkin fold. This stately design can be used to cover and keep warm a roll placed at each place setting, or you can use the top of the Crown as a container for anything you wish.

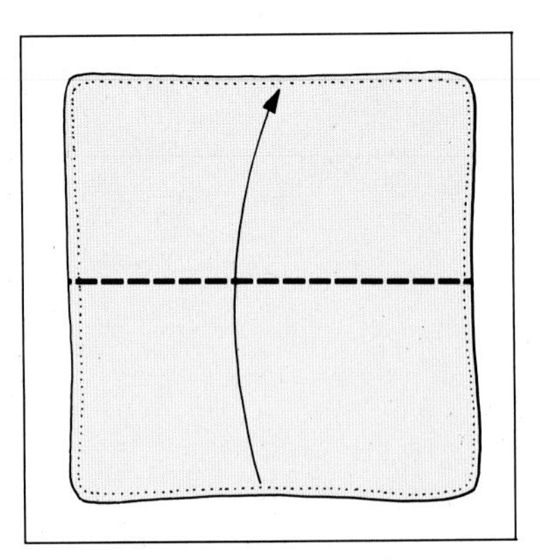

1. Begin with an open napkin. Fold the bottom edge up to the top edge.

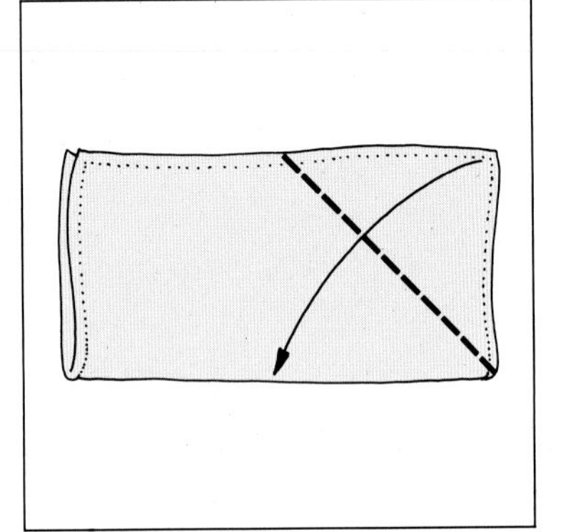

2. Fold the top right corners down to the bottom edge.

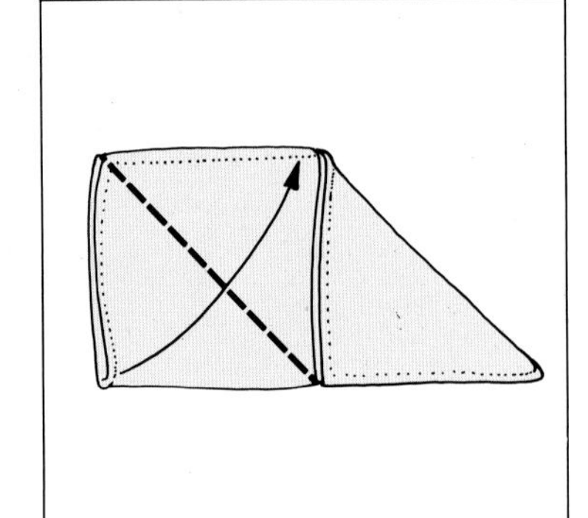

3. Fold the bottom left corner up to the top edge.

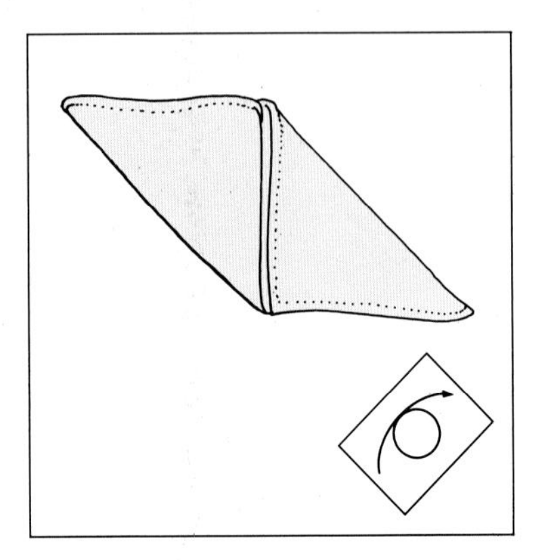

4. Turn the napkin over and position it so that the long folded edges are at the top and bottom.

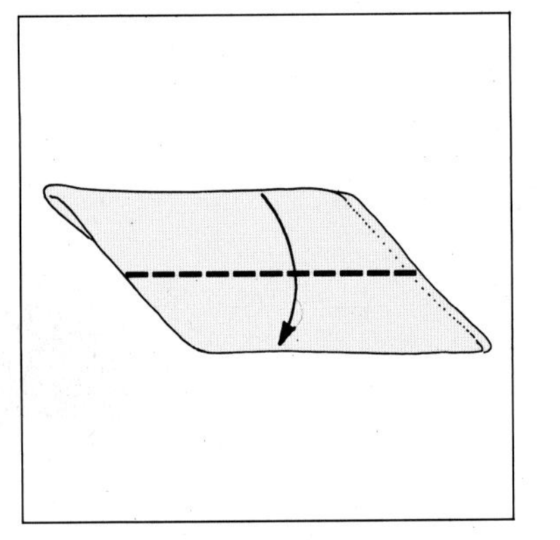

5. Fold the top edge down to the bottom edge.

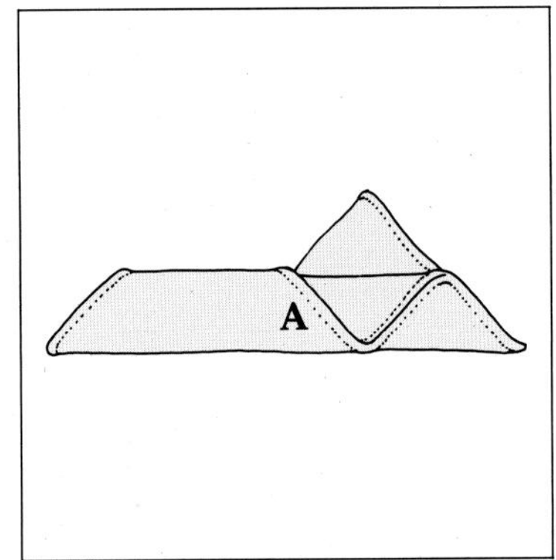

6. Slip a finger under edge A and slide it upward to release the hidden point (see drawing 7).

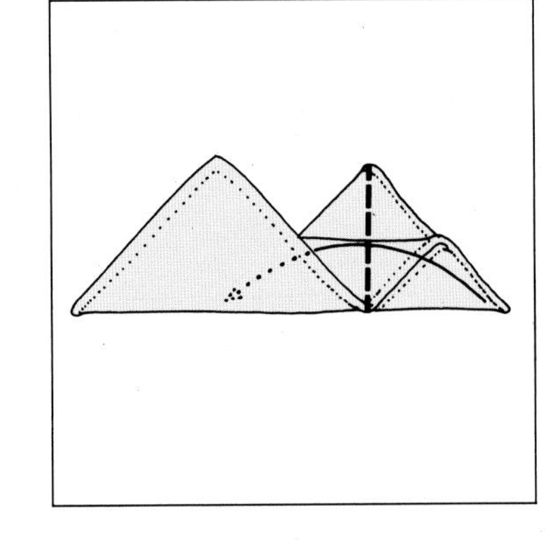

7. Bring the right bottom point over to the left and tuck it under the edge (see drawing 8).

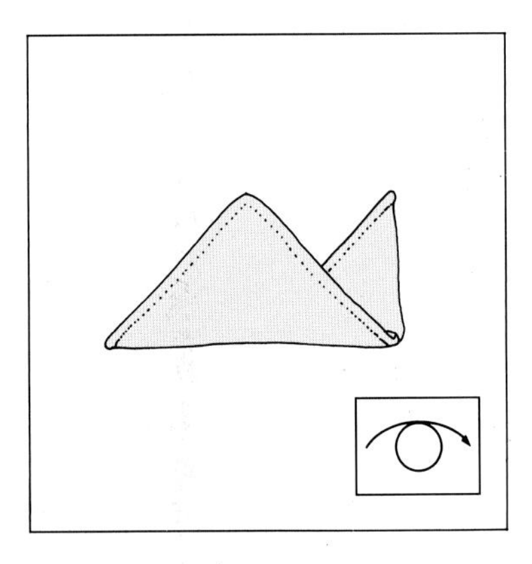

8. Turn the napkin over.

© Tony Cenicola

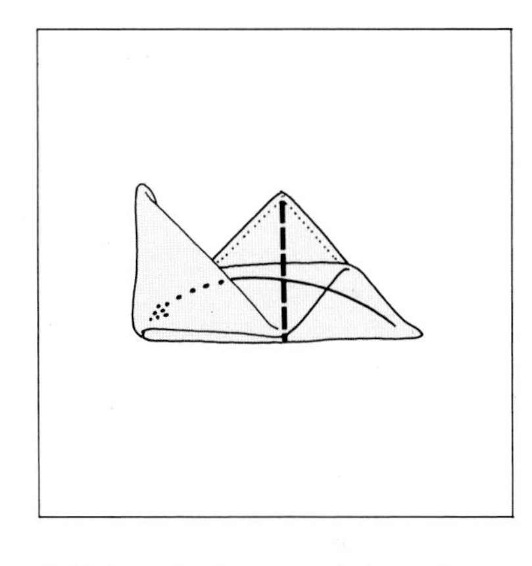

9. Bring the bottom right point over to the left and tuck it into the pocket.

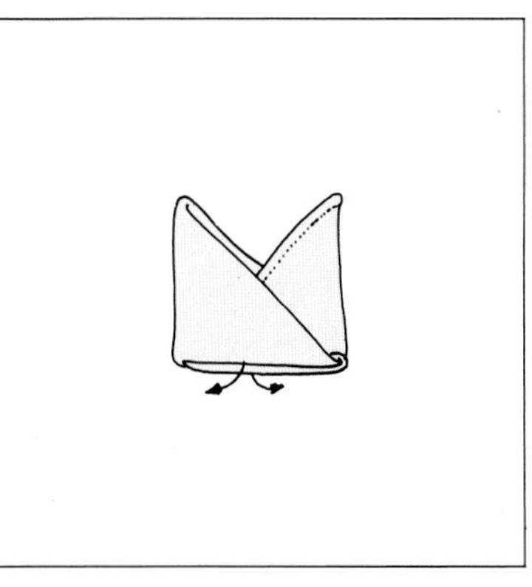

10. Open the Crown at the bottom and pull the edges apart to give it a round shape.

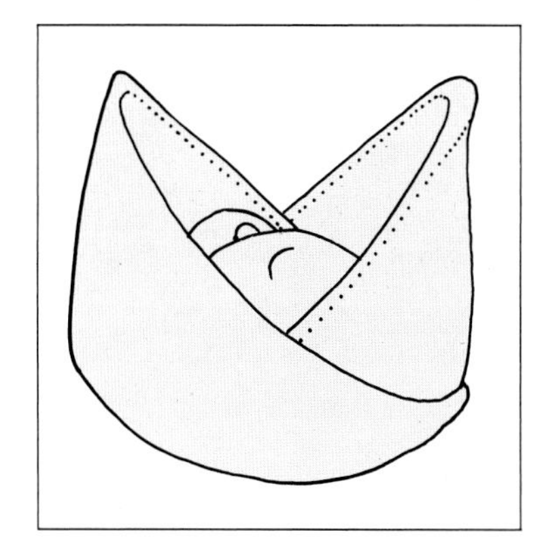

11. Stand the completed Crown on a plate or on the table.

LEAF

(Design by the author)

Celebrate spring or fall with this Leaf design.
The Leaf will stay better if a cloth napkin is used.

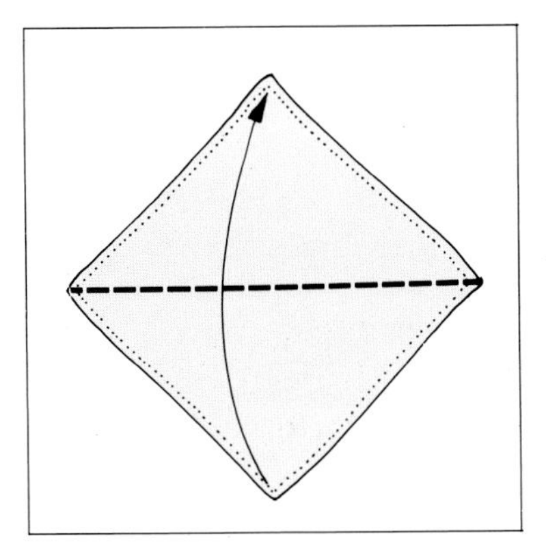

1. Begin with an open, square napkin in the shape of a diamond. Bring the bottom point up to the top point.

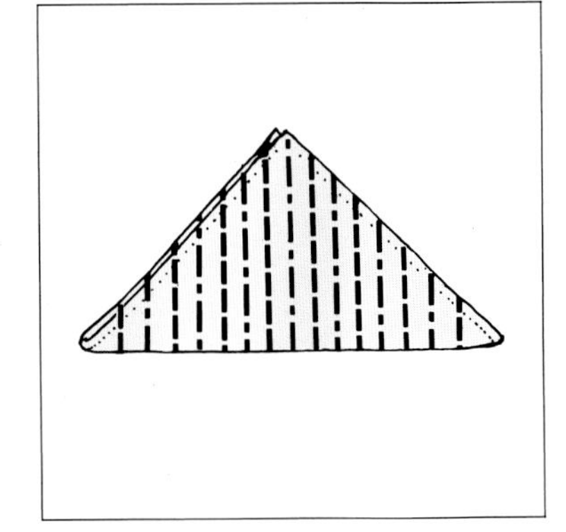

2. Beginning at one side corner, accordion-pleat the napkin across to the opposite corner.

3. Unfold the center pleat. (You may want to count the number of pleats to find the center pleat.)

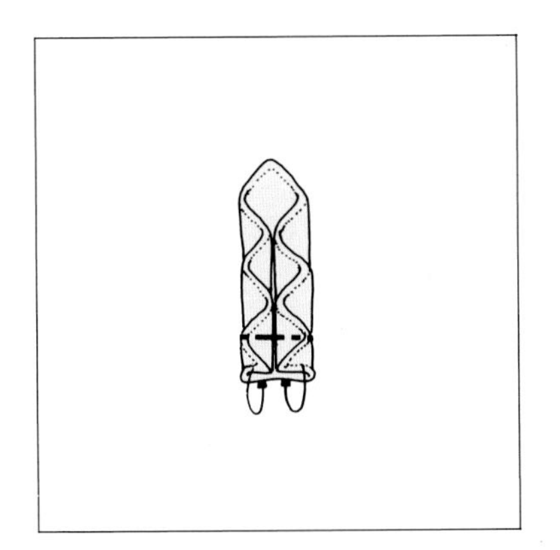

4. Hold the napkin so that the two piles of pleats are lying side by side. Fold back the bottom end of the pleats.

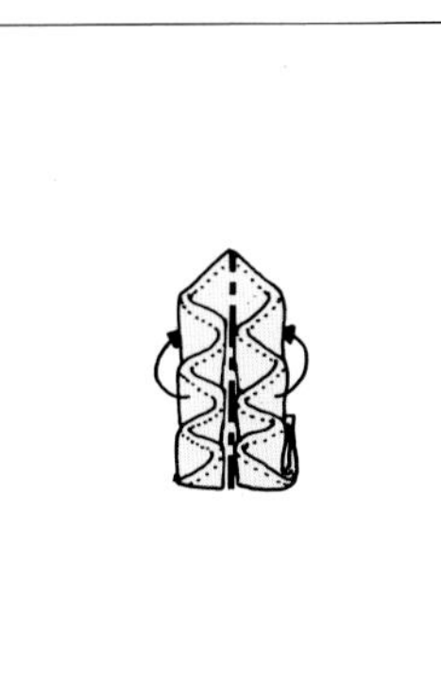

5. Fold the right and left piles of pleats backward to meet behind. (You are refolding on the center pleat.)

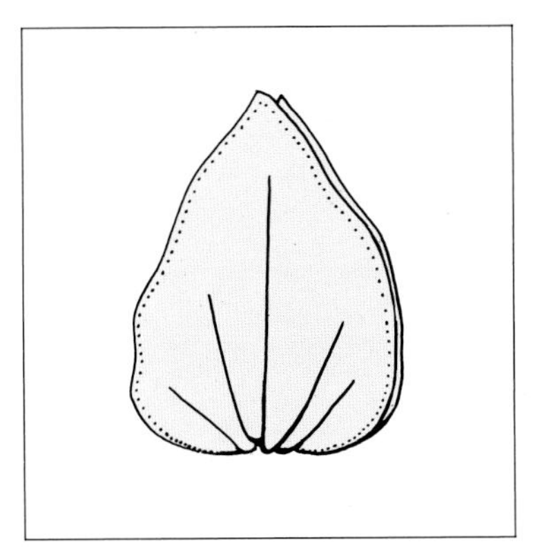

6. Shape the completed Leaf and lay flat on the table or on a plate.

STANDING FAN

Often seen in restaurants or cruise ships, this dressy fan design is always appealing. Use a sturdy napkin that will hold its shape; cloth is best.

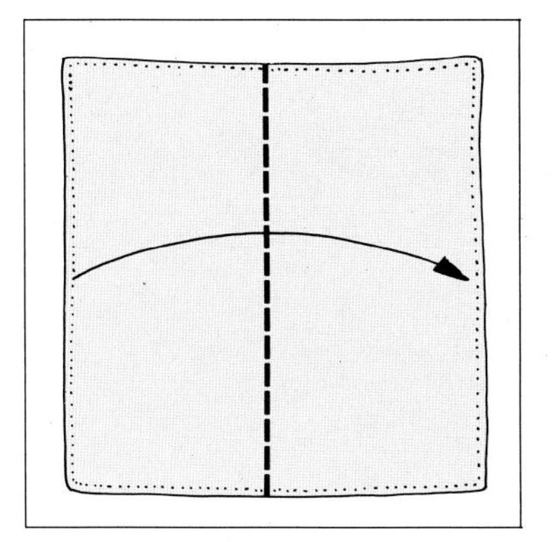

1. Begin with an open napkin. Fold the napkin in half, from left to right.

2. Beginning at the bottom edge, accordion-pleat two-thirds of the way toward the top edge.

3. The pleats you just made should be behind the bottom edge. Fold the napkin in half from right to left; the pleats should now be on the outside.

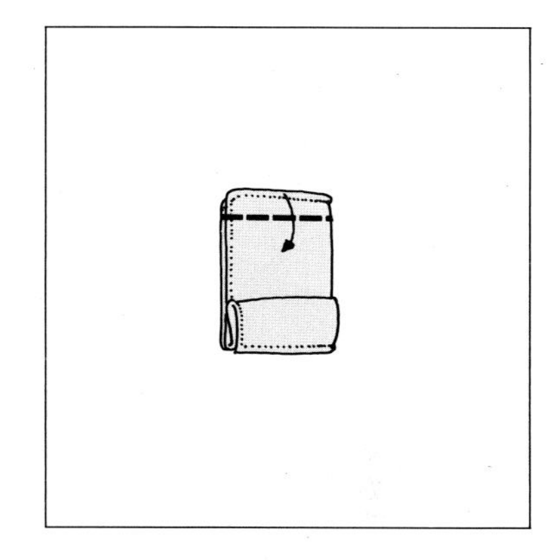

4. Fold the top edge of the napkin down to form a small hem.

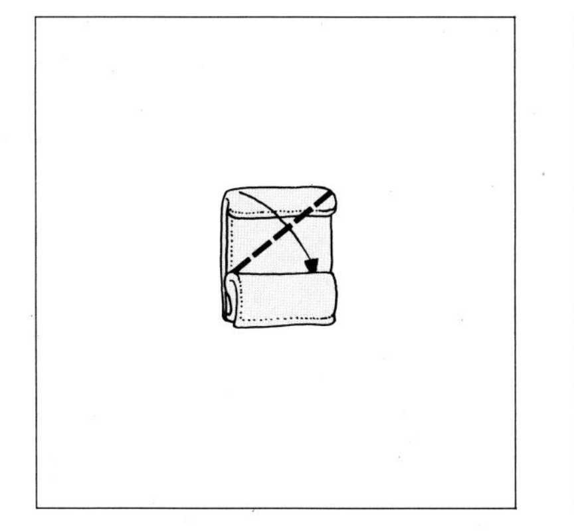

5. Fold the left side of the napkin down diagonally and tuck it behind the pleats. (If this edge does not fit neatly behind the pleats, go back to step 4 and adjust the size of the hem you made.)

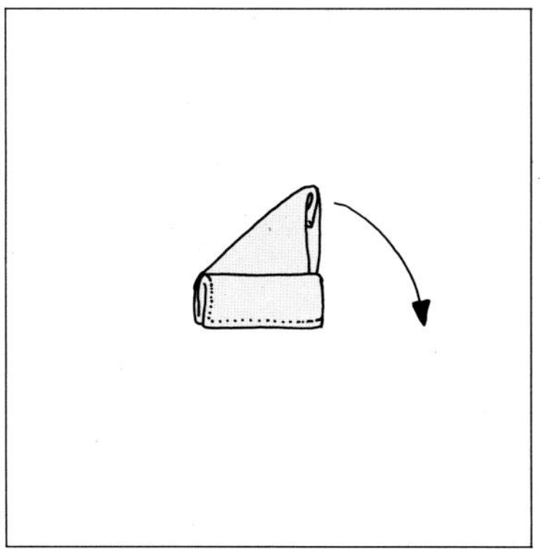

6. Stand the napkin on the right edge.

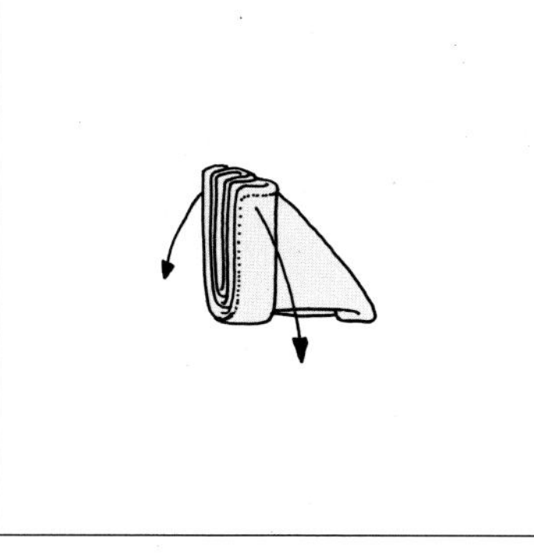

7. Release the fan.

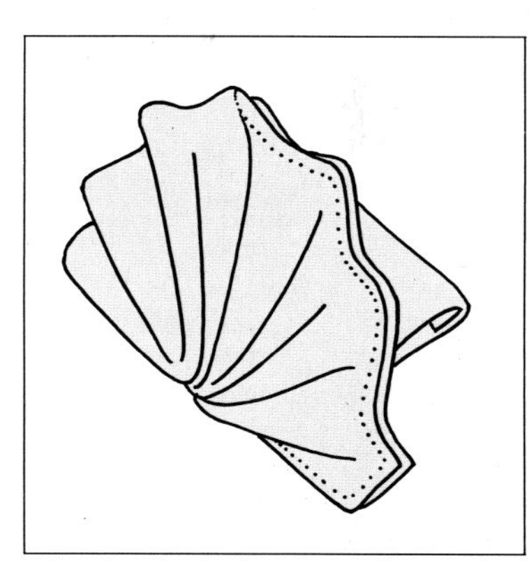

8. Completed Standing Fan.

SWAN

This delightful Swan should be folded from a square paper napkin. For best results make sharp creases. This fold may take a little practice to perfect.

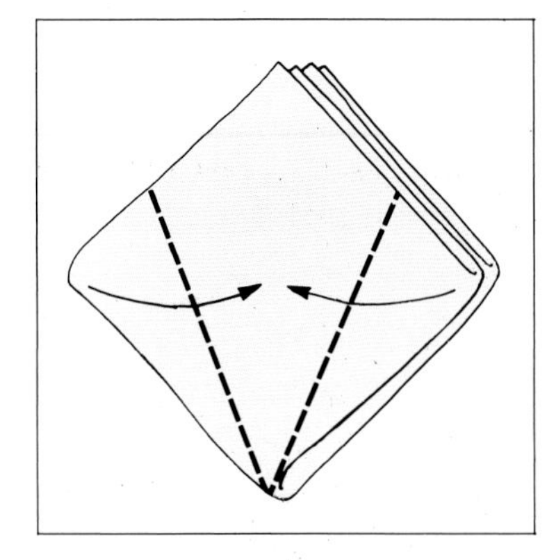

1. Begin with a napkin folded into quarters. Position the napkin so that the four free corners are at the top. Fold the bottom side edges in to meet at center.

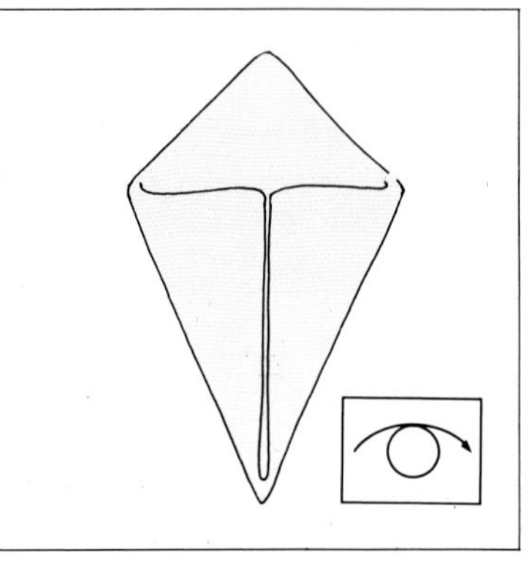

2. Turn the napkin over, keeping the sharp point at the bottom.

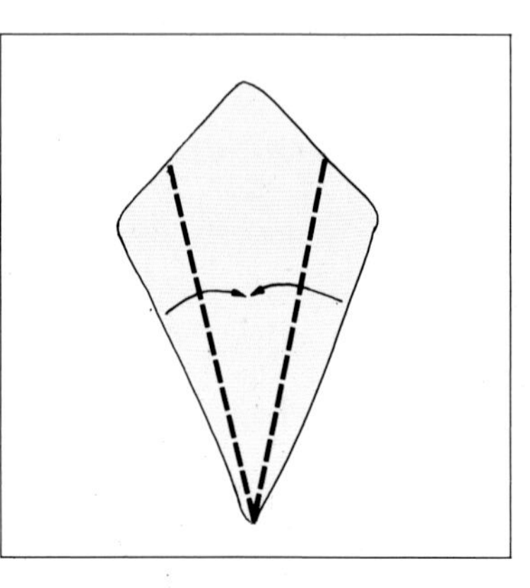

3. Narrow the sharp point by folding the long sides in to meet at the center.

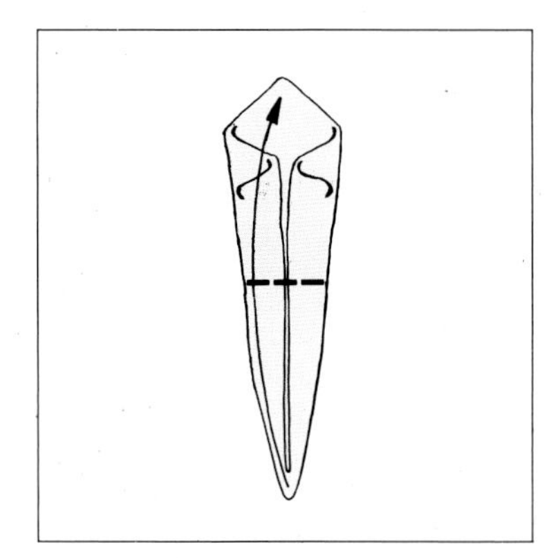

4. Fold the bottom point up to the top point.

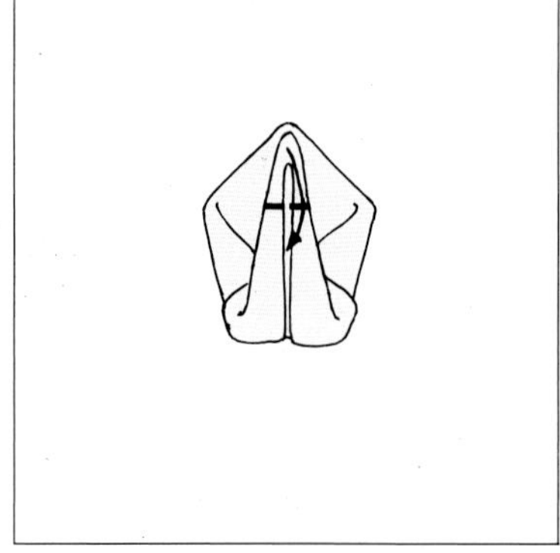

5. Fold the sharp point down a little to form the head.

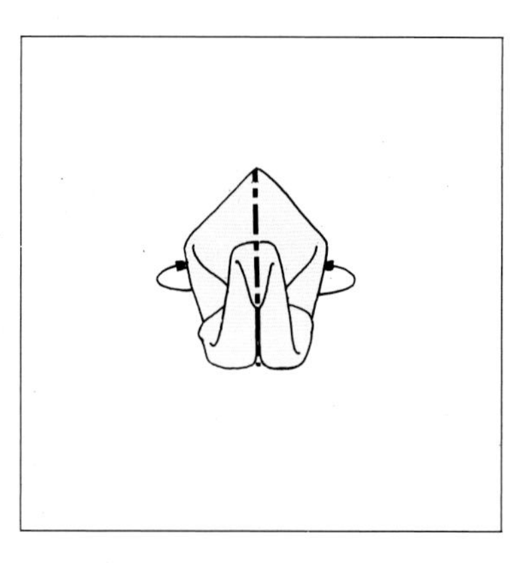

6. Fold the napkin in half along the center line so that the right and left sides go backward. (The head will remain on the outside.)

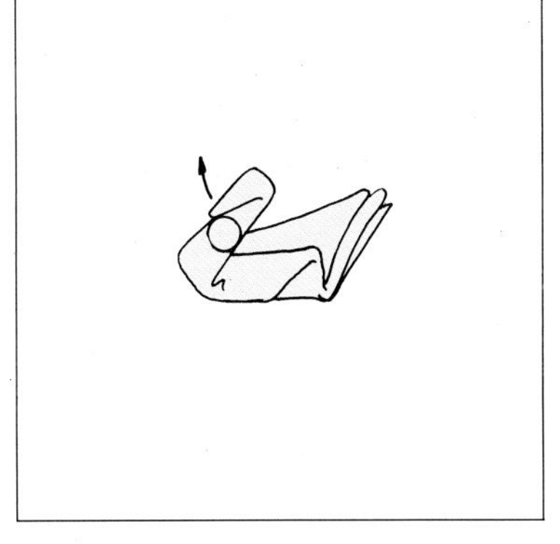

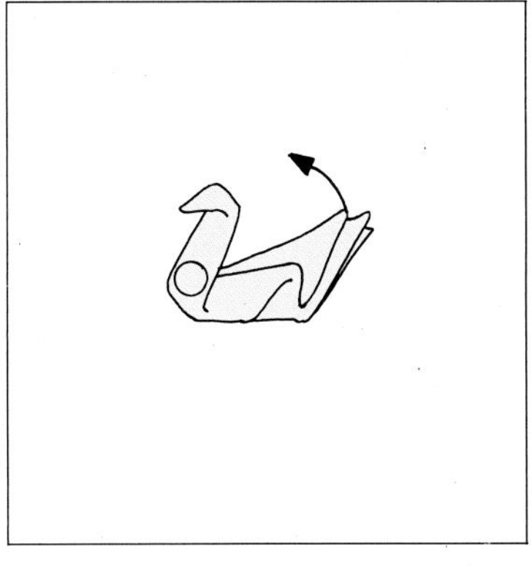

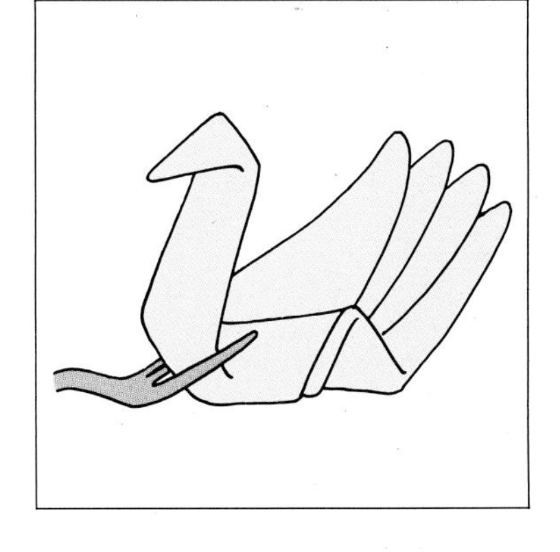

7. Rotate the napkin to the position shown and hold it at the circle. With your other hand lift the neck slightly and pinch it near the base to lock it in place.

8. Hold the neck at the circle. With your other hand lift the head away from the neck and pinch it in place where the head and neck connect.

9. Hold the swan at the base of the neck. There should be several layers of paper at the tail end of the swan. Carefully pull up each individual layer and separate them slightly to form a "fluffy" tail.

10. To keep the swan from spreading apart, insert the tines of a fork into the front end of the swan (at the base of the neck), or tie a thin piece of ribbon around the neck.

WATER LILY

The layers of petals and lovely flower shape make the Water Lily a traditional favorite. Use it as is to adorn your table, or as a container to hold a roll, a small crock of soup, or even nuts. This design will work best if folded from a stiff napkin.

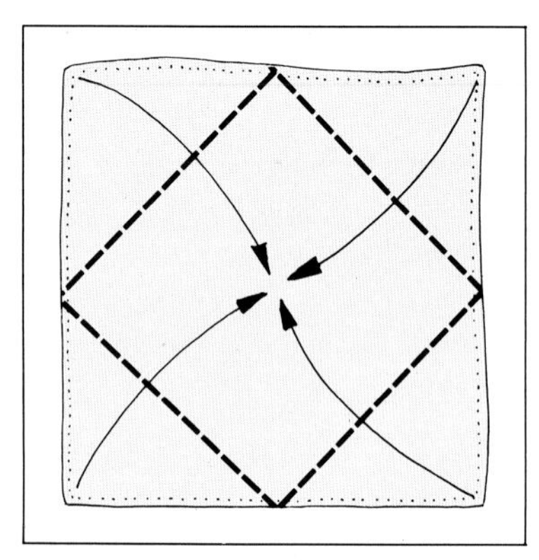

1. Begin with an open, square napkin. Bring all four corners inward to meet at the center.

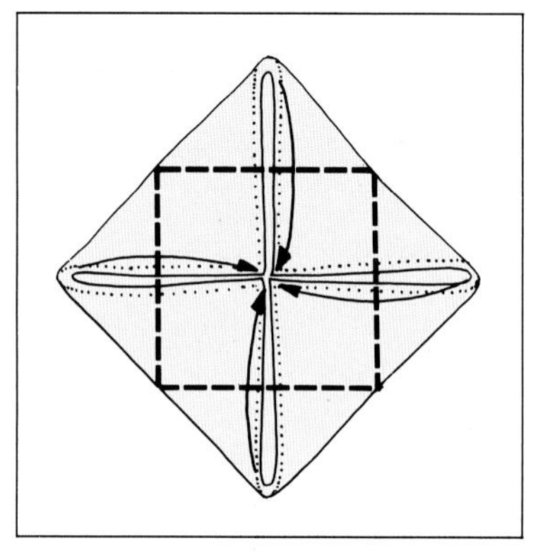

2. Fold each outside corner in to meet at the center.

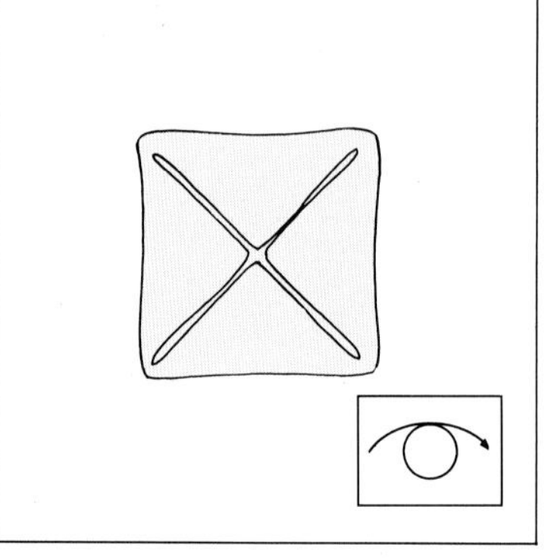

3. While you hold the center points in place with one hand, slip your other hand underneath the napkin and carefully flip it over to the back.

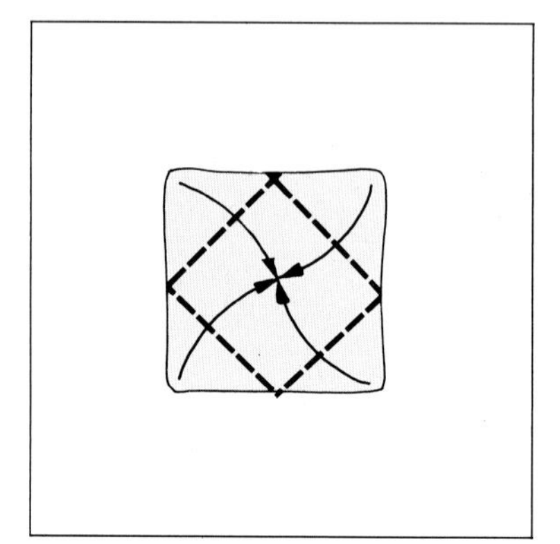

4. Fold each outside corner in to the center.

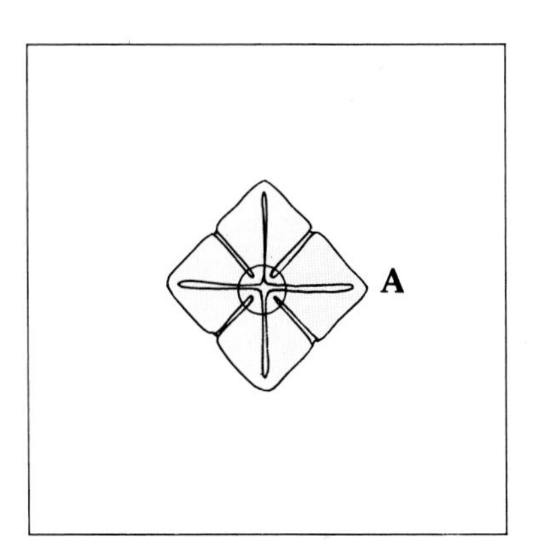

5. While doing this next step, it is very important that you keep the center points you just folded securely in place, either by holding them down with your hand or by placing a glass on top of them. Starting at one outside corner (A), slip your free hand underneath the napkin and pull out one of the loose corners from the underside of the napkin.

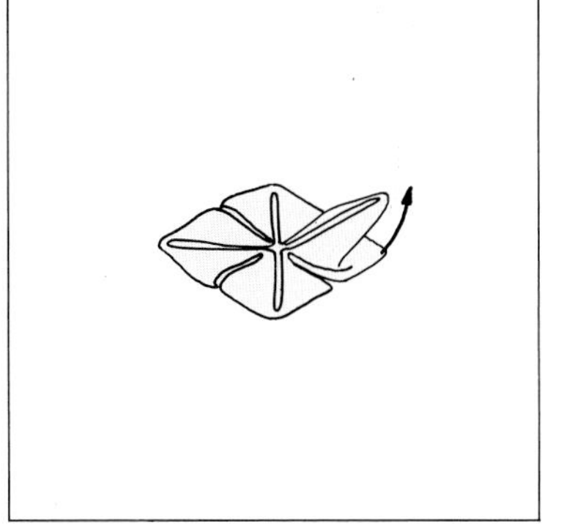

Pull this corner out and upward so that it softly wraps itself around corner A to form the shape of a petal (see drawing 6).

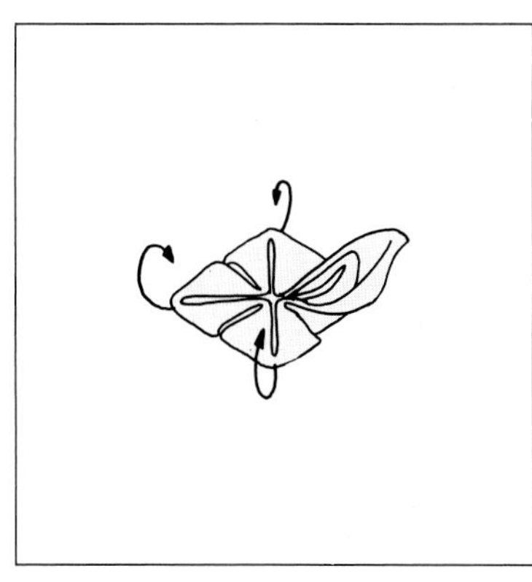

6. Repeat step 5 on the other three corners. Remember to keep the center points firmly in place.

7. Slip your hand under side B and pull out the loose corner from under the napkin. Pull the corner upward and tug at it gently.

8. Repeat step 7 on the three remaining corners from the underside of the napkin. If your napkin is stiff enough, it will form a soft cup shape.

9. Completed Water Lily.

Variation: If you are using a very large or limp napkin, you may wish to add an extra layer of petals to your flower. Repeat step 2 before turning the napkin over at step 3. After step 8 there will be four more loose corners underneath that can be pulled out and upward. Your finished flower will be smaller and will hold its shape better.

CHAPTER THREE

Designs to Use With a Napkin Ring or a Glass

© Tony Cenicola

BOUQUET

Create the illusion of a bouquet of flowers at every place setting with this very simple napkin fold and a napkin ring.

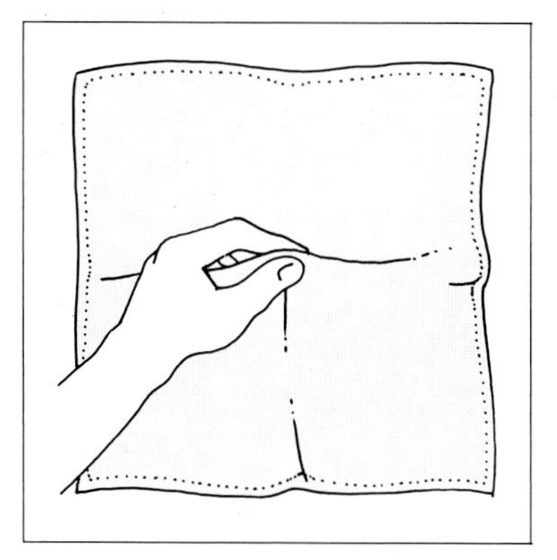

1. Begin with an open napkin. Hold the very center of the napkin and lift it in the air, letting the rest of the napkin hang loosely in soft folds.

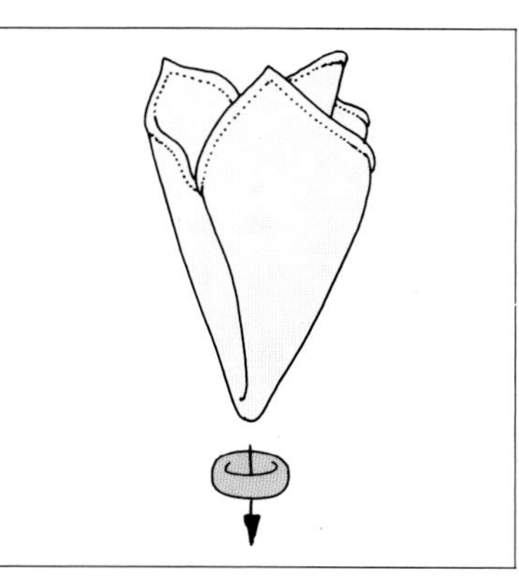

2. Slip the closed end of the napkin you are holding in your hand into a napkin ring and slide the ring down a few inches.

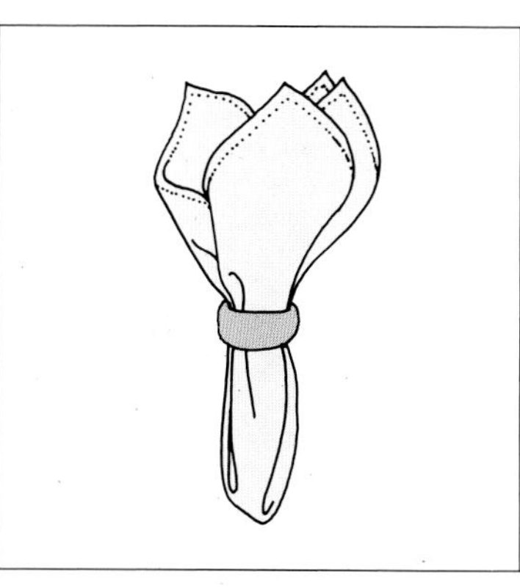

3. Shape the napkin for a pretty Bouquet.

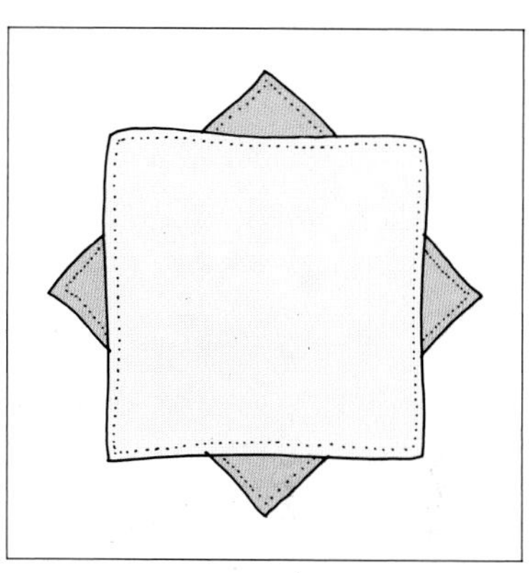

Variation: For a fuller and more colorful Bouquet, start with two napkins placed one on top of the other.

CACTUS

(Design by Susan Kalish)

The graceful leaves of this design add style to any table setting. Use a cloth napkin and a napkin ring with a wide opening.

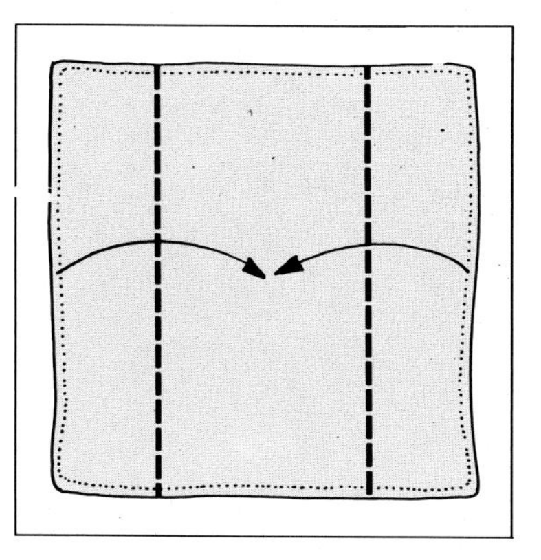

1. Begin with an open, square napkin. Fold the right and left sides in to meet at the center.

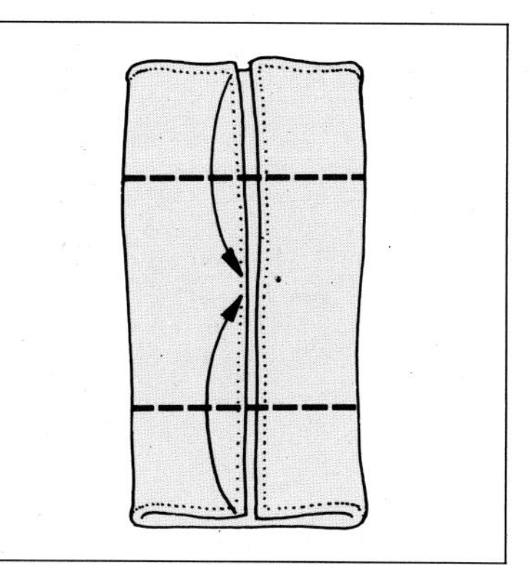

2. Fold the top and bottom edges in to meet at the center.

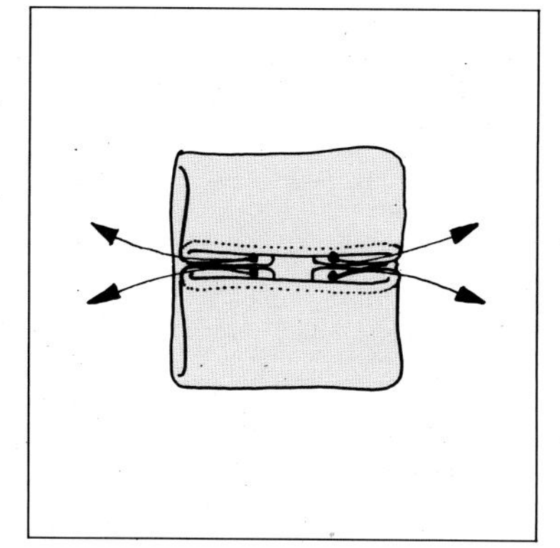

3. Look under the layers where the edges meet at the center: You will see four loose corners. One at a time, pull each corner out to the side. Each corner will form a point, as shown in drawing 4.

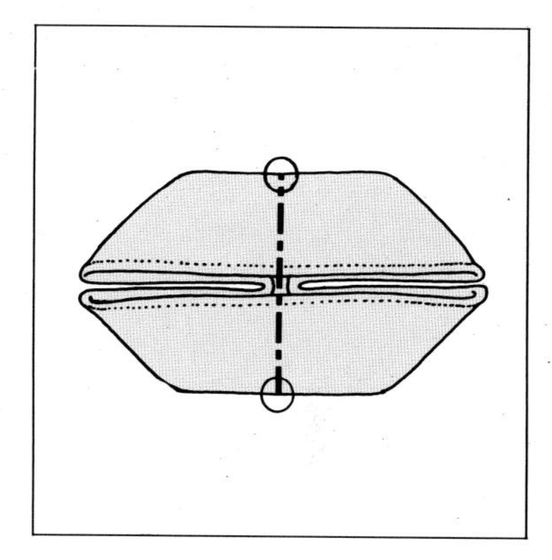

4. Lift the napkin at the center of the top and bottom edges and let the points hang down so that it folds in half backward. Lay the napkin back on the table and turn it so that all the points are at the top.

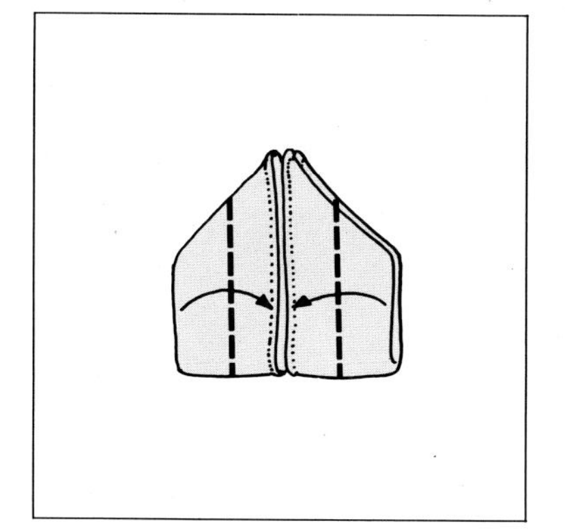

5. Fold the side edges in to meet at the center.

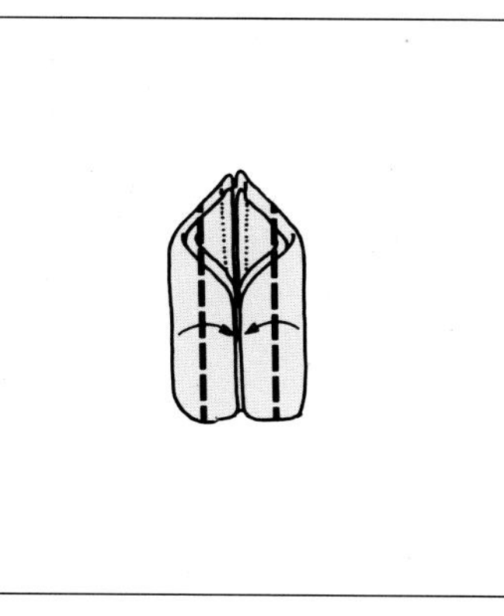

6. Narrow the napkin again by folding the side edges to the center.

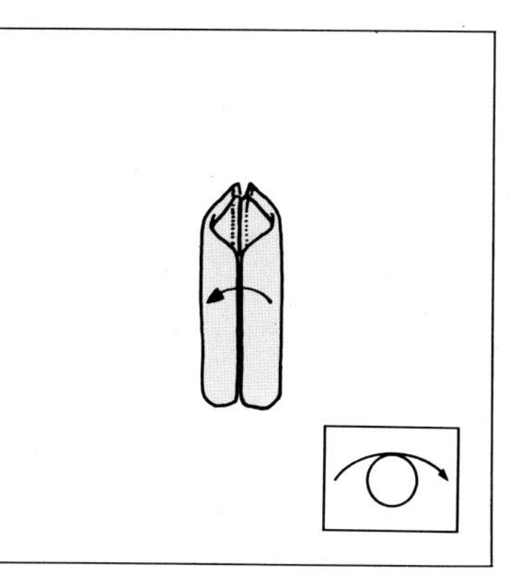

7. Fold the napkin in half and turn it over.

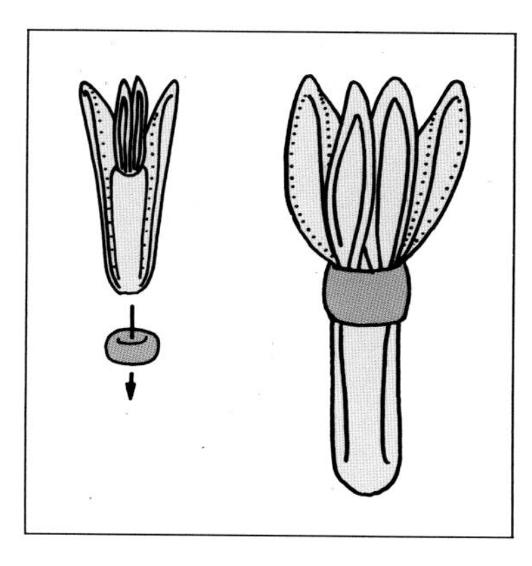

8. Insert the bottom end into a napkin ring and push the ring up a few inches, then shape the leaves of the Cactus.

CANDY CANE

This festive fold is made from two different colored napkins. You can match the colors to go with a specific holiday theme, or just pick two colors that look good together. Paper napkins are fine for this design.

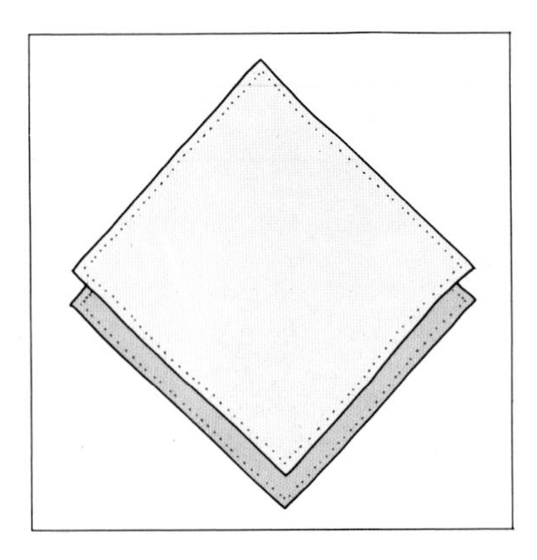

1. Place one open napkin over the other. The top napkin should be slightly higher, creating a V-shaped border approximately one inch (2.5 cm) wide.

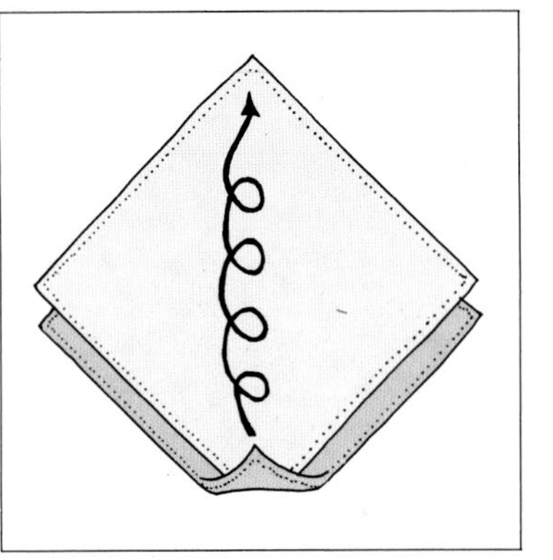

2. Beginning at the bottom corner, roll both napkins together toward the top corner.

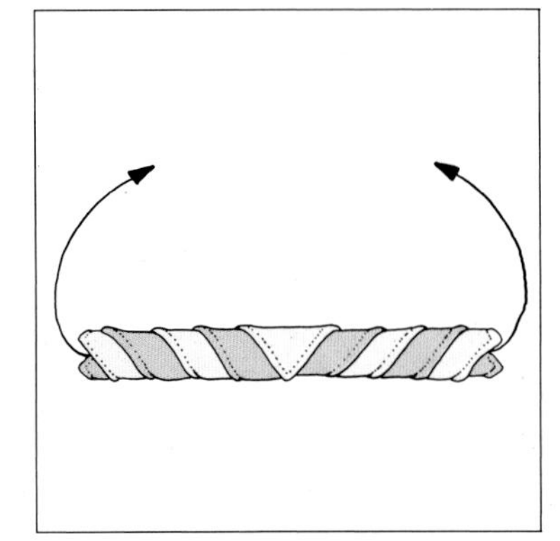

3. Your roll should have a striped design similar to a candy cane. Bring the opposite ends of the roll together, loosely folding the roll in half.

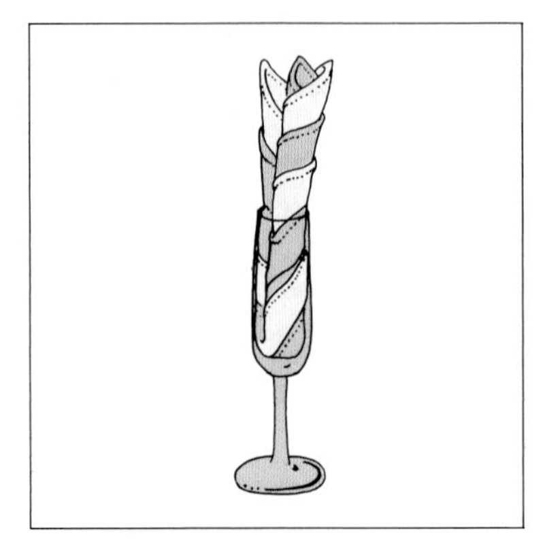

4. Insert the folded edge of the roll into a glass.

FAN

In Japan, the spreading fan is regarded as a symbol of growing prosperity and good fortune ahead. It is frequently depicted in their decorative arts and used for celebratory occasions. For variety, place the fold in a tall glass instead of in a napkin ring.

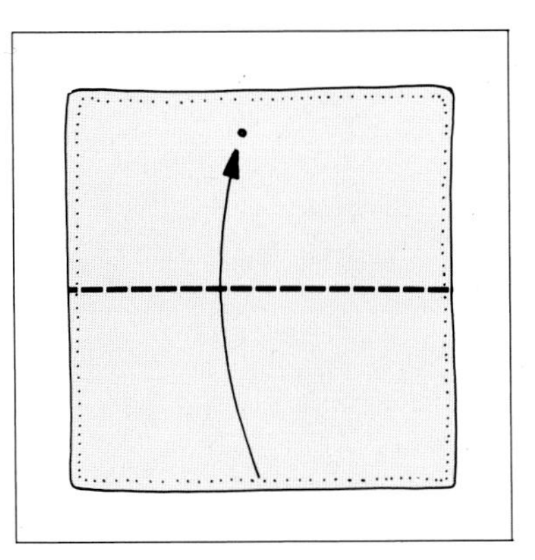

1. Begin with an open napkin. Fold the bottom edge up so that it lies slightly below the top edge. (Note: If you are using a napkin with a printed pattern, fold the bottom edge all the way to the top edge.)

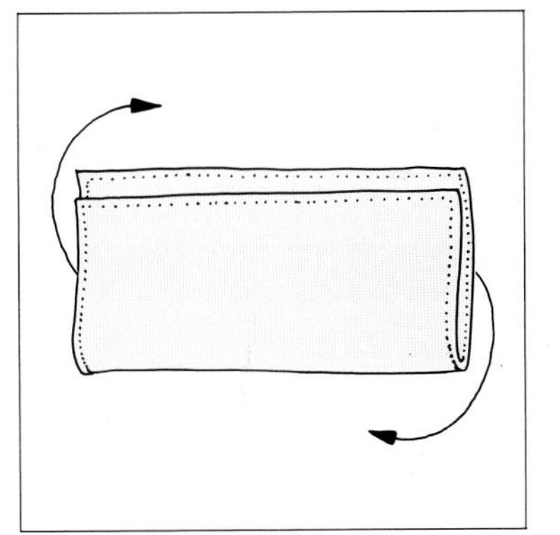

2. Rotate the napkin so that the side edges become the top and bottom edges.

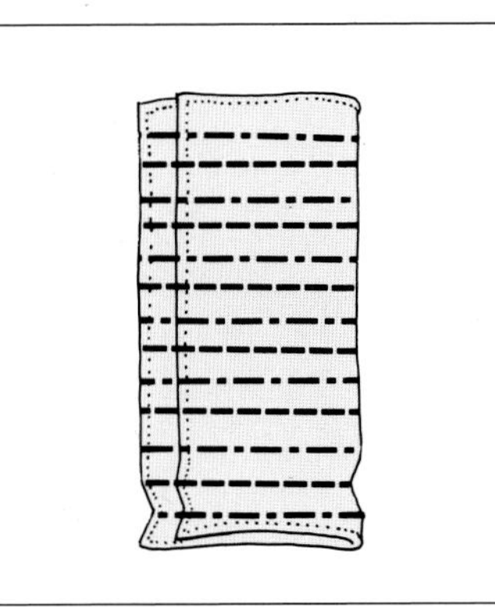

3. Beginning at the bottom edge, accordion-pleat the napkin up to the top edge.

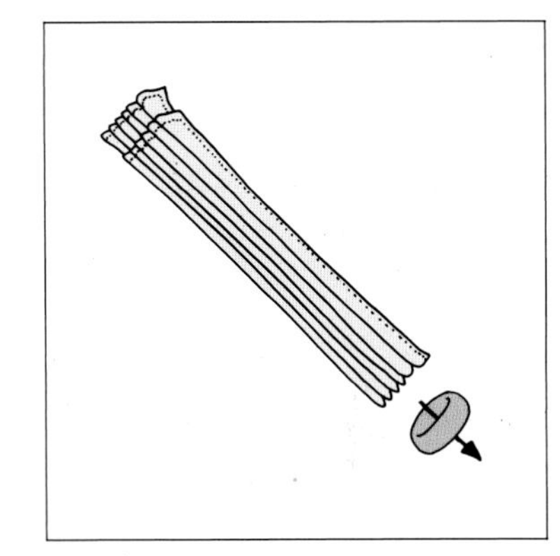

4. Insert a napkin ring onto the right end of the napkin. The napkin ring can be left near the bottom of the pleated napkin, or you can slide it furthur up, depending on how much you would like your fan to spread.

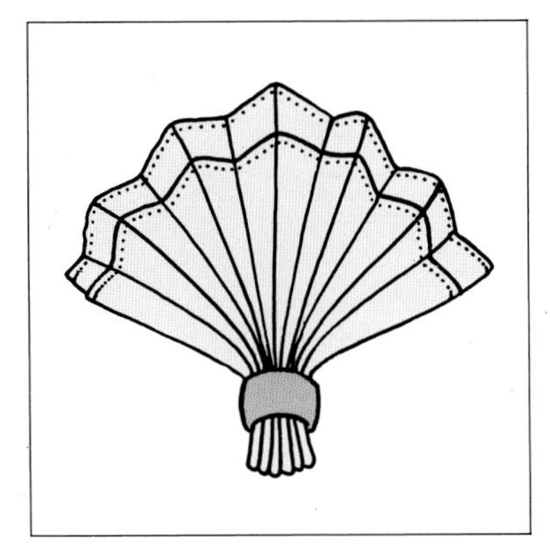

5. Place the napkin on a plate and spread the top pleats to form a Fan.

IRIS

The Iris design can be grand or dainty, depending on the size and type of napkin used.

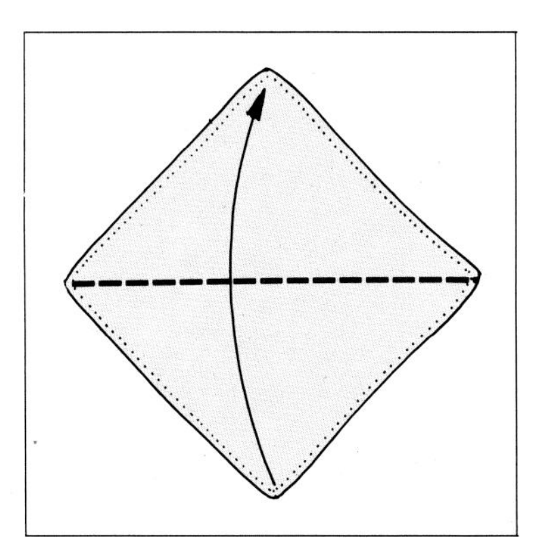

1. Begin with an open, square napkin placed on the table in the shape of a diamond. Fold the bottom point up to the top point.

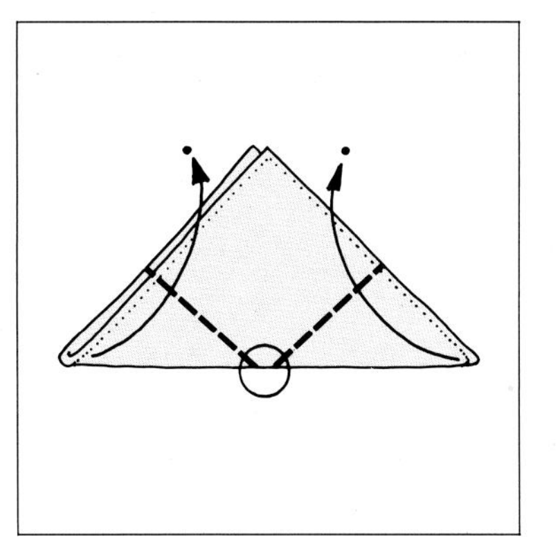

2. Hold your finger at the center of the bottom edge as you fold up the left and right points so that they are at the same height as, but slightly to the sides of, the center point (see drawing 3).

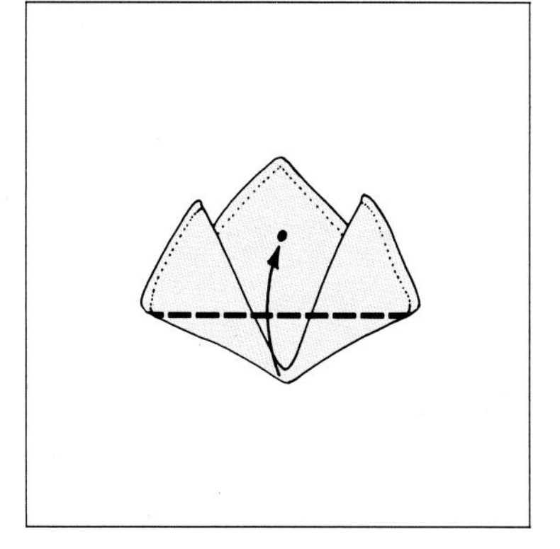

3. Fold the bottom point up as shown.

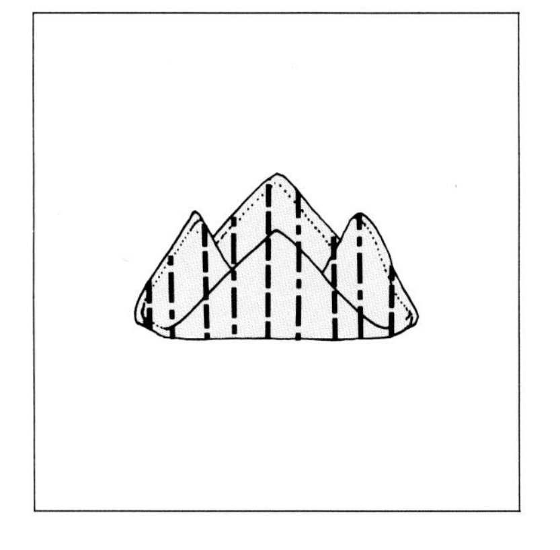

4. Beginning at one side, accordion-pleat the napkin across to the opposite side.

5. Place the base of the napkin in a glass (if the napkin is cloth) or insert between the tines of a fork (if the napkin is paper). Spread out the sides to form petals.

ROSETTE

The Rosette is a very showy design, especially when made from brightly colored napkins.

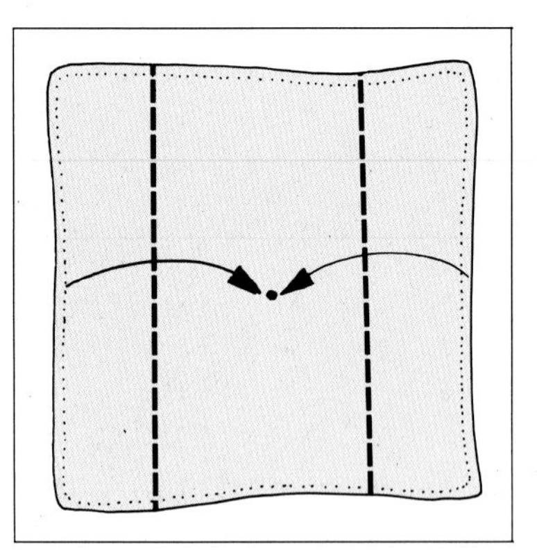

1. Begin with an open napkin. Fold the right and left sides in to meet at the center.

2. Starting at the bottom edge, accordion-pleat the napkin up to the top edge.

3. Tie a narrow ribbon around the center of the napkin (or use a very narrow ring). Lay the fan on a plate and let the pleats fan out into a full circle.

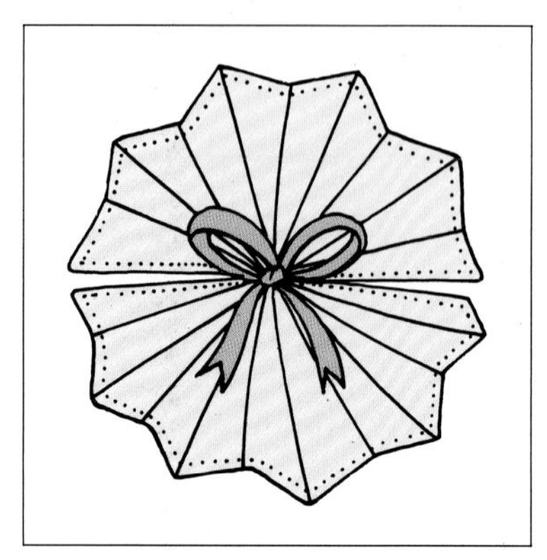

4. Completed Rosette.

CHAPTER FOUR

Table Service Designs

CRACKER HOLDER

Aside from crackers, this clever basket can also be used to serve wrapped candies, packets of sugar, or other small table fare. A cloth napkin is required for this fold. This is not an easy fold and may take several attempts to perfect.

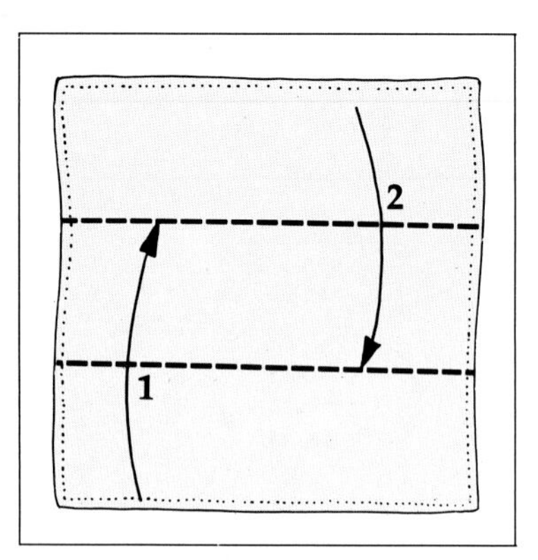

1. Begin with an open napkin. Fold the napkin in thirds, as you would fold a letter.

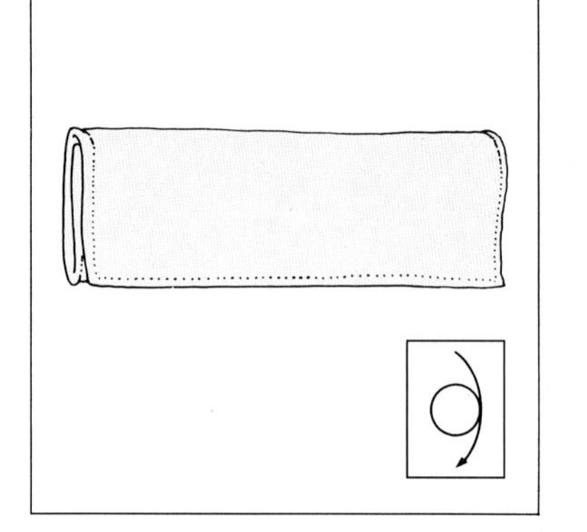

2. Turn the napkin over.

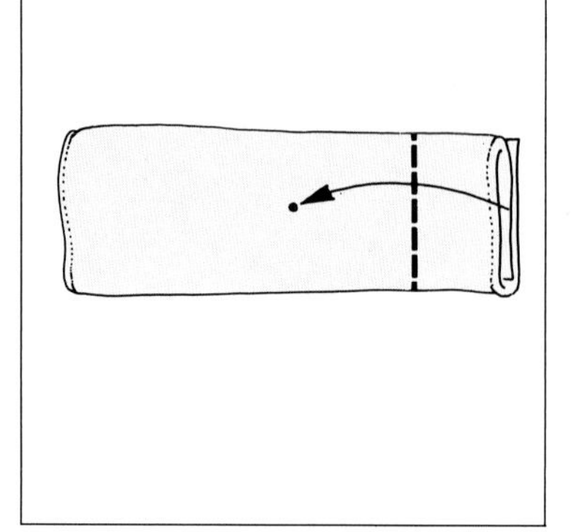

3. Fold the right side edge to the center. (This is a temporary fold that serves as a guide for the next step. It is unfolded in step 5.)

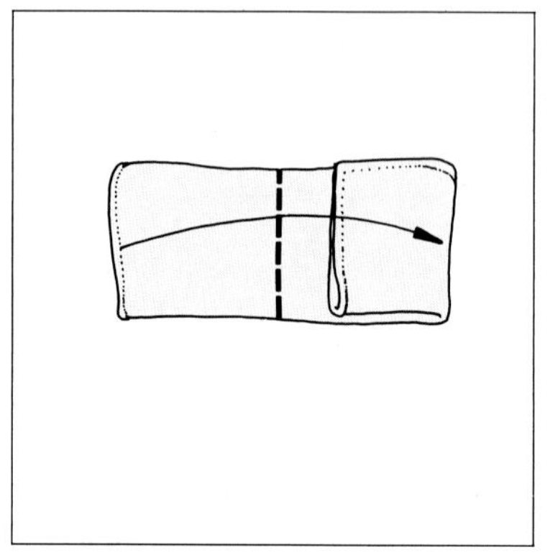

4. Bring the left edge to the far right edge.

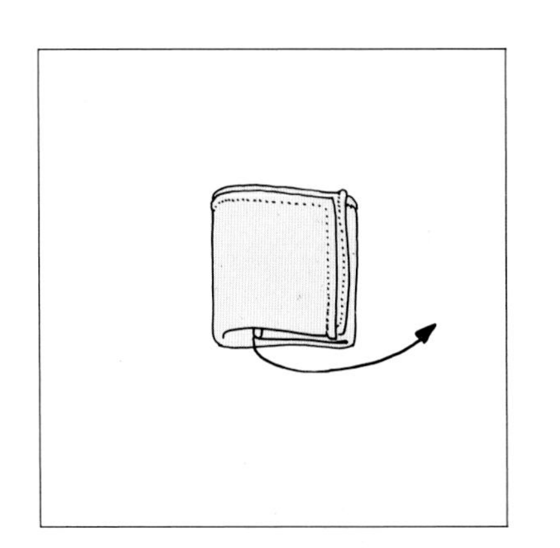

5. Reach under the flap you just folded over and unfold the flap you folded over in step 3.

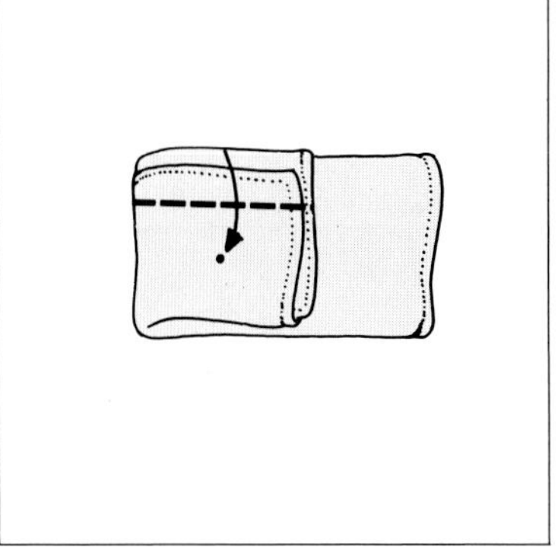

6. Lift the top edge of the flap and fold it down one-third of the way. As you do this, the top left corner will squash down and form a small triangle (see drawing 7).

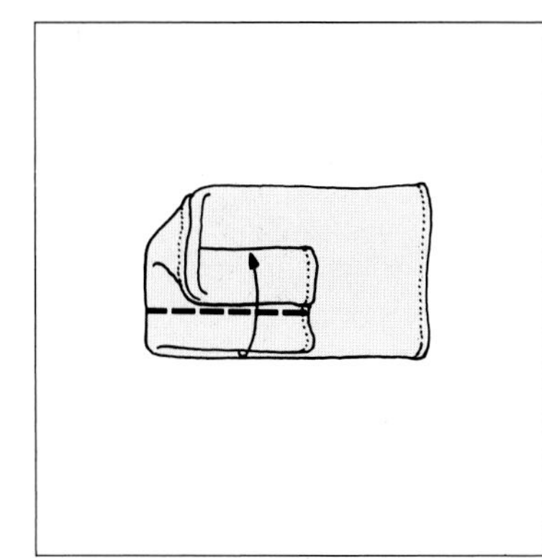

7. Repeat step 6 at the bottom of the flap.

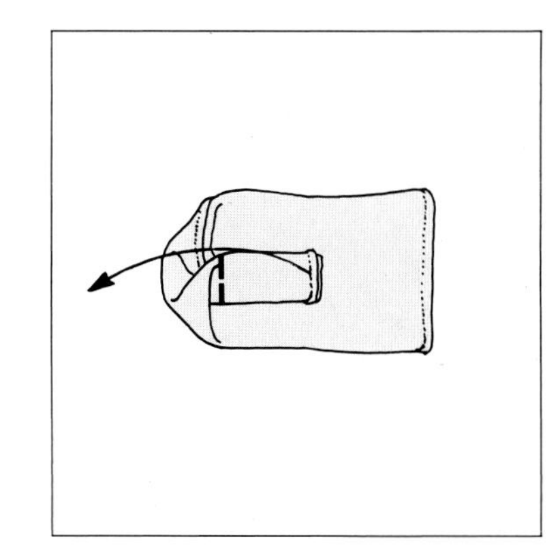

8. You now have a narrow flap extending from two small triangles. At the base of the triangles, fold the flap over to the left.

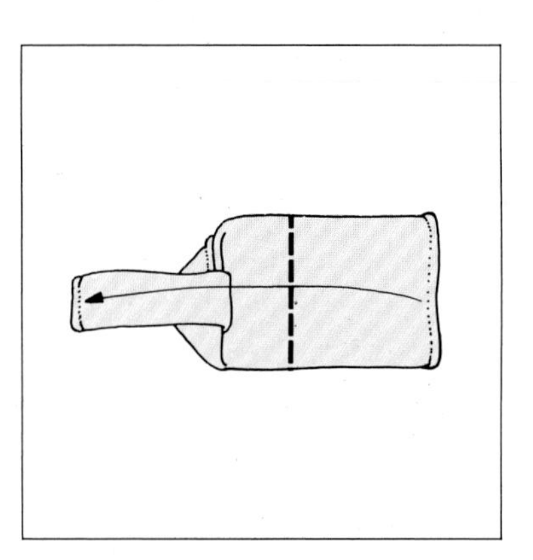

9. Fold the right edge over to the left edge of the narrowed flap.

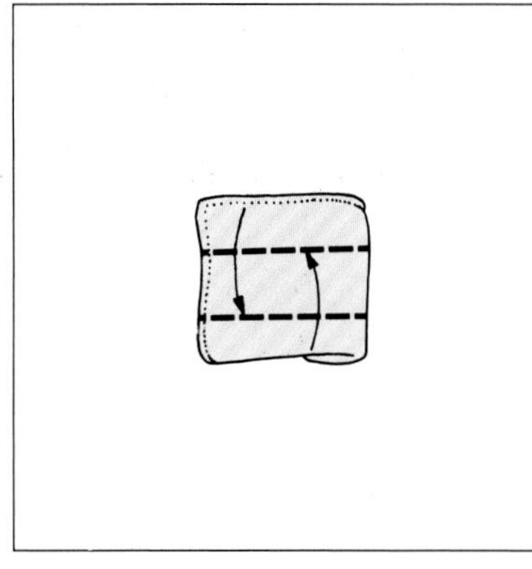

10. Repeat steps 6 to 8 on the right side.

11. Hold at edges A and B and turn the napkin inside out. The flaps that are now extending out to the sides will fall inside and line a rectangular-shape basket.

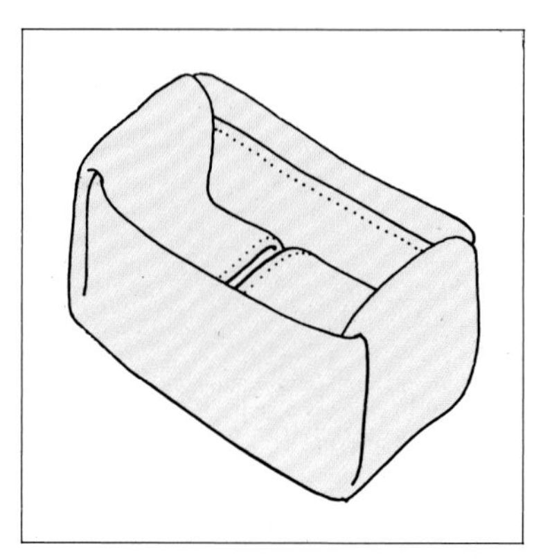

12. Completed Cracker Holder. Shape the basket by pressing your fingers into the bottom corners and straightening the sides and lining.

HOT STUFF

(Adapted by the author)

This simple fold turns a single-layered napkin into a compact, multilayered pocket. Use it as a pot holder or as a trivet. It is suitable for use with hot dishes, but should not be used for things taken directly from the oven. Fold from a heavy cloth napkin. If you are using a napkin with a printed pattern, begin with the patterned side facing up.

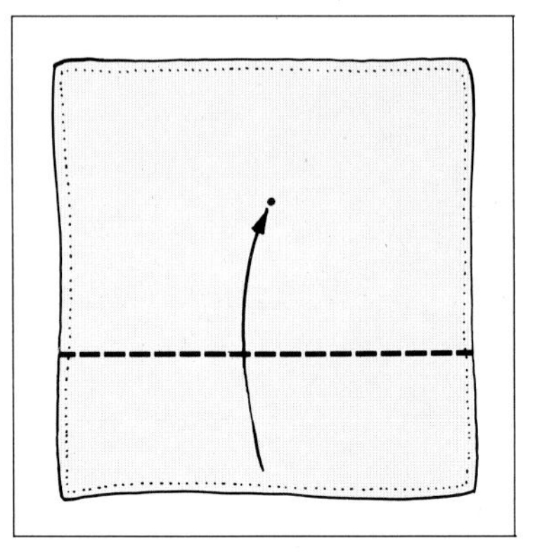

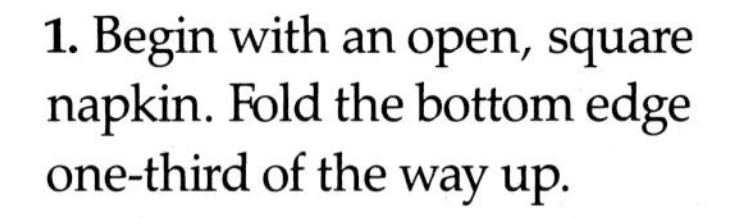

1. Begin with an open, square napkin. Fold the bottom edge one-third of the way up.

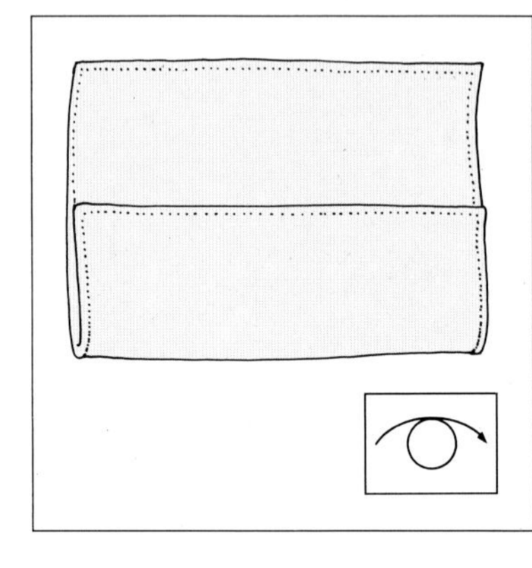

2. Turn the napkin over.

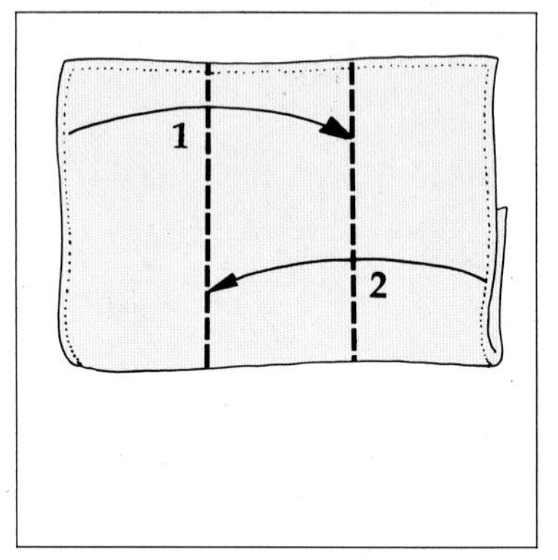

3. Fold the napkin in thirds, as shown.

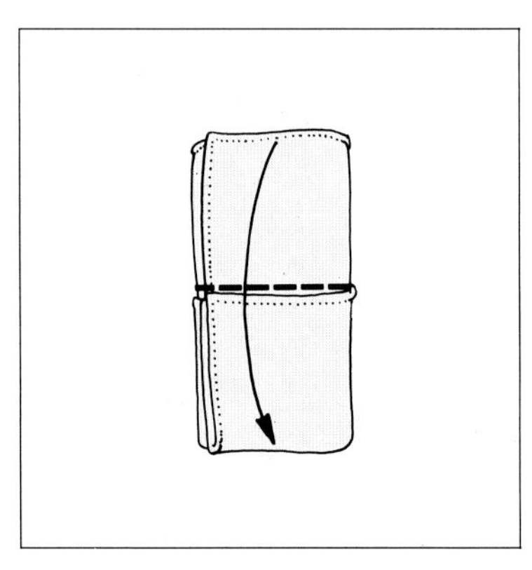

4. Fold the top edges down to the bottom.

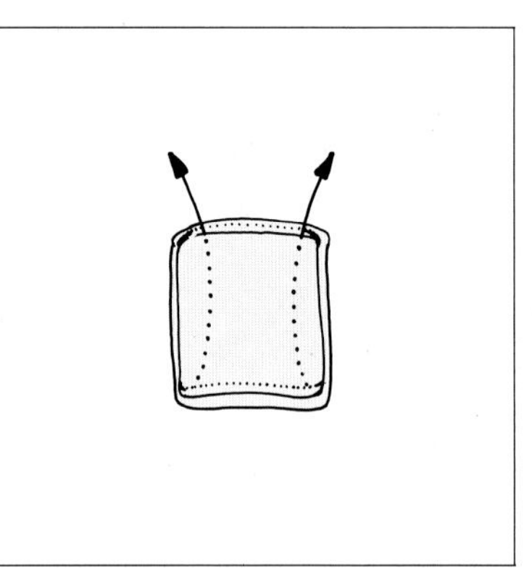

5. At the top edge of the napkin is a pocket. Insert your hands into the right and left sides of the pocket, leaving your thumbs on the outside. Turn the napkin inside out (like a glove).

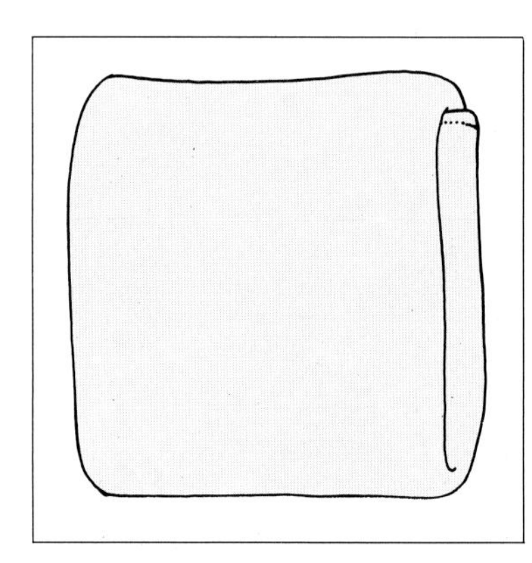

6. Neaten the corners of the pouch by poking your fingers down to the bottom corners and your pot holder or hot plate is complete.

PLACEMAT

Here's a design you can use as a placemat when folded from a large cloth napkin. As with Hot Stuff, if you are using a napkin with a pattern, make sure the patterned side is facing up.

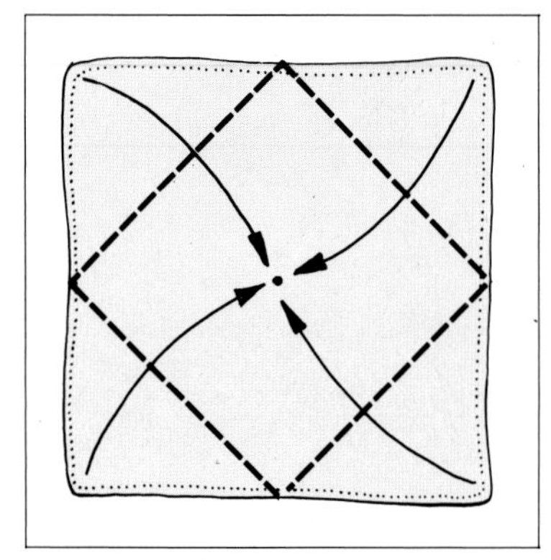

1. Begin with an open, square napkin. Bring all four corners in to meet at the center.

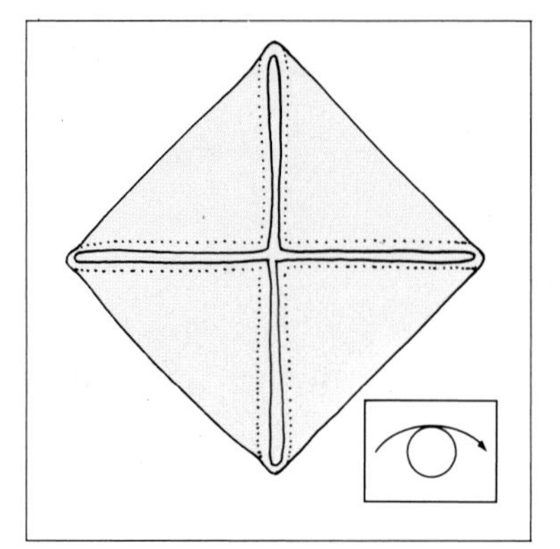

2. Hold down the center points with one hand, and carefully turn the napkin over.

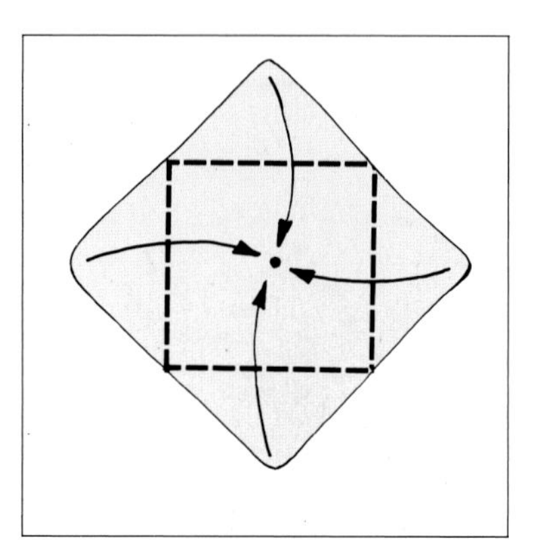

3. Bring all four outside corners in to meet at the center.

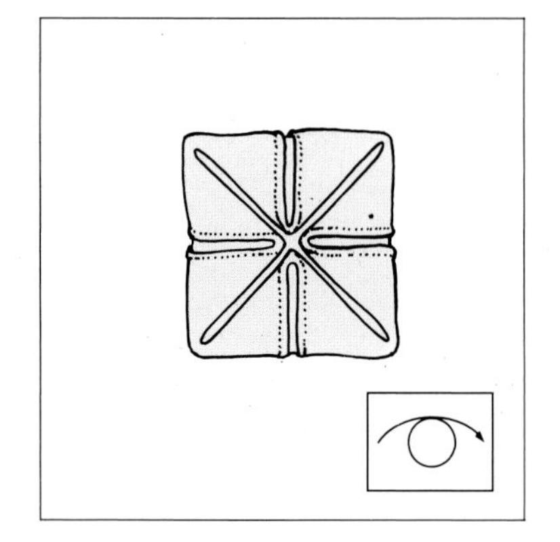

4. Carefully turn the napkin over.

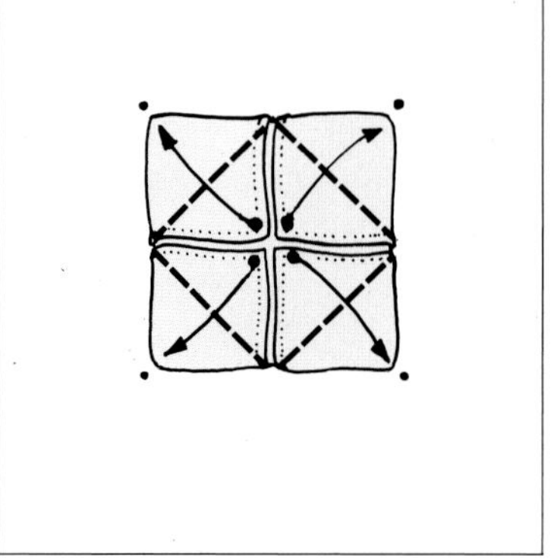

5. Take one of the inside corners and fold it out to the nearest outside corner. Tug at it slightly to help keep it in place. Repeat with the other three inside corners.

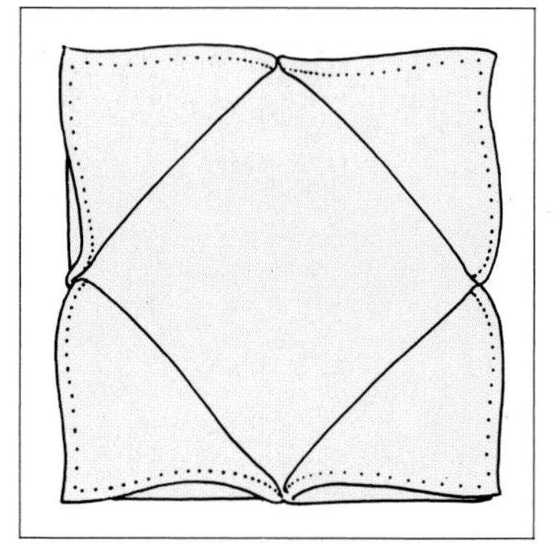

6. Your completed Placemat will probably fit well under a small luncheon plate.

PICTURE INDEX

This index will help you select the best napkin fold for any occasion. Just choose the design you want by looking at the finished result here, then turn to the corresponding page for folding instructions.